Energy Vampires

A PRACTICAL GUIDE FOR PSYCHIC SELF-PROTECTION

Energy Vampires

A PRACTICAL GUIDE FOR PSYCHIC SELF-PROTECTION

Dorothy Harbour

Destiny Books
Rochester, Vermont

Destiny Books
One Park Street
Rochester, Vermont 05767
www.InnerTraditions.com

Destiny Books is a division of Inner Traditions International

Originally published in German under the title *Achtung, Energie-Vampire*
Copyright © 1999 by Econ Ullstein List Verlag GmbH & Co. KG, Munich
English translation copyright © 2002 by Inner Traditions International

LIBRARY OF CONGRESS CATALOGING-IN-PUBLICATION DATA
Harbour, Dorothy.
[Achtung, Energie-Vampire. English]
Energy vampires : a practical guide to psychic protection / Dorothy
Harbour.
p. cm.
ISBN 978-0-89281-910-2
1. Self-defense—Psychic aspects. 2. Vital force. I. Title.
BF1045.S46 H3713 2002
133—dc21
2001007912

Printed and bound in the United States at Lake Book Manufacturing, Inc.

10   9   8   7

Text design and layout by Virginia L. Scott Bowman
This book was typeset in Galliard with Helvetica Narrow as the display typeface

Contents

PART THREE
*Protection against Energy Vampires in
Business and the Workplace   107*

Introduction

In the mid-1980s I dared to step into an unusual existence. Practically overnight I decided to quit my job with an insurance company to open a practice for spiritual energy and life consulting. At that time, there were no role models in my life for this sort of undertaking. On the contrary, spiritual questions did not seem to matter much to the people in my office with whom I spent the better part of my days, nor to my friends and acquaintances. Instead, these people seemed to be in constant competition over material goods and their careers, and money, wealth, and power.

Their lust for power and material goods only strengthened my conviction that people in reality were hungry for something: something that is scarce in the physical world, and thus constantly fought over. And, as I knew from years of personal experience, this essential "something" was the energy of life. Although different cultures and eras have called this energy *ether, prana,* or *chi,* it is uniformly viewed as the universal energy of life, a resource that is infinite on the spiritual level.

During the 1980s, I made a connection between the energy of life and the longing for power and profits—based on my own experience with energy. Like so many people during their first years of life, as a small child I had a sensitivity, which in other cultures may also have been common among adults. Without noticing that I was "doing" anything special, I could intuitively sense the thoughts and feelings of those around me—the kinds of thoughts that remained unspoken and the kinds of feelings people tried to hide. I also possessed an ability for which modern science is only now beginning to discover the biochemical foundations: just as all of us can see the brightness around the sun, as a young girl I saw the brightness—or, to use a broader expression, the aura—around every living person, every animal, and, on a lesser level, every plant.

Unlike other children, I did not lose these abilities as I grew older. Although harsh teasing and social pressure taught me to hide my "strange" abilities from others, my fascination with these spiritual talents was stronger than my wish to fit in with others. Whatever my educators tried to tell me, I've known throughout my life that they were wrong about one important point: living beings don't resemble sharply delineated sculptures, but rather angels and holy people of early paintings, who are usually surrounded by auras of rays, or even depicted as bodies of light.

Chapter 2 goes into more depth about what this aura is and how you, or anyone, can learn to see the energy fields surrounding living beings. But at this point, I will explain a few fundamental truths.

Every person is surrounded by a protective shell of pure energy. Even though today's adults are not usually able to spontaneously recognize the aura of living beings, the findings of modern science confirm the existence of such energy fields, as well as their inherent visibility. Our eyes have certain receptors with which we can see the rainbow-colored aura. These receptors can be activated through training, primarily by using simple focusing techniques, which many past societies have utilized as part of their cultural norm. The modern worldview has continued to narrow perception to the point where only the material world and the so-called laws of nature have come to be accepted as reality. Each person is so strictly socialized that most of us no longer "believe our eyes" and can see only what is considered visible by predominant views. As contemporary science begins to recognize the existence of energy fields, more and more of us are regaining our capacity to see them.

EVERYTHING IS ENERGY

At the dawn of the third Christian millennium, the realization is beginning to settle in that there is no real contradiction between the ancient concept of a universal energy, from which all life flows, and scientific knowledge.

According to physicists, matter can be transformed into energy (and vice versa), and any one kind of energy can be transformed into any other kind. Thus, we accept that wind energy or water energy can be transformed into electrical energy, which in turn can be turned into heat energy, and so on. In addition to these nonliving realms of our physical reality, we have come to use a similar definition in other areas of our lives as well. We speak of "sexual energy," of the "energetic appearance" of a determined individual and also of "criminal energy." These phrases express the widespread and correct conviction that all of these energies are different aspects of a single cosmic force, which influences all of creation—every single living being as well as the things we consider to be inanimate.

In contrast to the physical forces of wind, water, and electrical energy, we are currently able to control and transform life energy only in very limited degrees, if at all. The problems begin with the simple measurement of life energy: the electrical currents that stimulate organisms often occur in such low doses that even the most sophisticated machines are unable to measure them, or to measure them accurately. And what about the powerful life energies that continue to escape technical definition and measurement? For example, no one would doubt the presence and powerful nature of sexual energy, but who would ever be able to measure this energy, which Sigmund Freud named libido? These problems only become more complex when we try to actively control the *transforma-tion* of the libido into spiritual, mental, or creative energies, a transformation that undoubtedly happens all the time, as we can see from the works of extraordinary and strong-minded individuals (holy people, wise people, and artists) of all eras.

The case is similar with the other forms that life energy can take, which up to the present time have been only vaguely defined. Who could deny that some people have a considerably stronger "presence" than others? But how can you measure such charismatic energy—or even manipulate it? With what means can we increase our *own* presence? And, in turn, how can we resist the charismatic energies of others, to protect ourselves from the energy rays of political crooks and overbearing salespeople? Do we have an energy immune system that we need to care for and strengthen just as much as our physical immune system? Did you ever consider that many victims in our society—of physical or sexual abuse, unemployment, social degradation, or bullying and acts of violence—in the end were all overcome by the same *energy vampires?*

INTRODUCING THE ENERGY VAMPIRE

Vampires don't exist only in scary novels. In fact, famed vampires such as Dracula likely represent only fantastic descriptions of their real-life counterparts who were energy vampires that lived not off the blood but off the life energy of their victims. At first, the term *energy vampire* may sound bizarre, even though it quite accurately describes the facts: psychological power over others can be obtained (and misused) only by those who can control internal life energy and are able to manipulate it. To put it in a positive light: those who can strengthen their internal life energy will not become victims of energy vampires, since they will not offer a vulnerable psyche upon which energy attackers may prey.

But what leads energy vampires to steal the life energy of their fellow humans in the first place? The answer to this question stems from what was previously said: in contrast to electrical energy, with which we can gain wind or water strength, most of us hardly know how to control and manipulate life energy in the physical world. A light of life energy burns in each living being, similar to the energy in combustion engines, that gives each living being the energy necessary for survival. But for an energy-deficient person to increase his or her energy level, the only available resource is the energy of a suitable, but insufficiently protected, fellow human.

People like myself, who are able to see the energy mantel that surrounds every individual, often see a familiar, but always disturbing, sight when we observe two people arguing with one another: both auras flow into one another and are colored orange to red at the crossing points. As soon as one of the combatants wins and the loser backs away, the two auras separate. The aura of the victor is notably inflated and has gained in volume as well as shine. In contrast, the aura of the loser seems to have shrunk, similar to a balloon that is losing air. The aggressor may think he feels great because he offered the better argument. In fact, the aggressor is drunk on the energy that he has taken from the opponent. By the same token, the loser feels downtrodden and exhausted; through this vampire attack, the loser has just lost part of his life energy. We would be much more careful and kind with one another in this society if more people were able to witness this impressive spectacle of energy robbing.

COMMON TYPES OF ENERGY VAMPIRES

Let us take a closer look at the three most common types of these energy robbers.

The Love Vampire

The most common cases of energy vampirism result from the fact that people have differing energy levels. In nearly every group or family, and in a significant number of marriages and other partnerships, there is an individual, who—rightfully or not—feels less vital than the rest of the group and thus tries to profit from the "energy riches" of the others. Everyone knows at least one of the most common type of energy thief among their group of friends. These thieves usually stick to small but repetitive attacks: they act as though they were always insulted or in need of consolation, and they crave attention. By receiving attention through manipulation, thieves share in the energy resources of others. Often, this strategy more or less works for extended periods of time, until one day the constantly "exhausted" partner or parent gets sick, collapses, flees, or announces the depletion of his or her energies in a similarly dramatic way.*

The Power Vampire

Dominating others, forcing an opinion on them, and manipulating their thoughts and actions are, for many, valid methods for feeling good, strong, and confident. In a similar fashion, power vampires get high on the power they exert over others. They pursue dominant roles at work and at home—as managers, as bosses of every rank, and as the one "wearing the pants"—and have others acting at their behest. Of course, we most often encounter power vampires in politics and in clubs and organizations that more readily dole out positions of power, more so than in other areas of life. The charisma that they project and that we often admire is usually the reflection of all the energy they have stolen from their admirers and subordinates. The overbearing salesperson who tries to sell you an overpriced product of questionable utility is often fol-lowing not only his desire for profits, but also his hope to tap the energy of his customer by exerting power. After all, money is nothing but a sym-bol for the flow of energy over which people are constantly fighting. It's no wonder that at the end of such an encounter we feel as empty and

---

*The love vampire appears in chapter 14 in its other guises: the charismatic hunter, the para-sitic homebody, and the energy beggar.

exhausted as our bank account. Our energy vampire, the salesperson, has feasted on our energy as well as our money.*

The Fear Vampire

We encounter psychologically ill or otherwise spiritually disturbed people more often than most of us might like to believe. Because their life energy is blocked, they try to tap the energy sources of others. They most often enter our psyches by instilling fears or doubts, leading us to doubt people we previously trusted, or ourselves and our abilities. Fear vampires often instill fear of possible conspiracies or other imminent catastrophes. Usually we can easily avoid contact with such people, and I strongly recommend avoiding any sort of emotional connection with them. But what if one's boss or colleague or even one's own partner turns out to be an energy vampire of this type?

WHO SHOULD READ THIS BOOK

This book seeks to outline the basic laws that govern the exchange of life energy and is thus aimed at all people interested in expanding their horizons and in developing their own potential to the fullest. The crux of the problem of energy vampires is not that there is a lack of life energy in the world; it is the sad fact that most people—whether they are vampires or victims—are not aware of their energy relationships. In fact, most actions in this area take place on a subconscious level, often leaving neither the victim nor the vampire with a clear idea of the dramatic events taking place. The dynamics of energy relationships and the sad presence of energy vampires are of particular relevance to people who find themselves in the following categories.

---

*I deal with energy vampires at the workplace in more detail in the third part of the book. Vampire salespersons are further discussed in chapter 12.

People Whose Psychological Shield Is Defective or Incomplete Due to Trauma

Damage to the aura—leaks, or places where energy cannot circulate freely—can be rooted in events far in the past, especially traumatic experiences in early childhood that have never been dealt with completely. But more recent spiritual and physical injuries—such as a painful separation or an accident from which we have only physically recovered—can damage our aura as well. This leads to energy vampires sensing easy prey—and stealing our life energy. Protect yourself from being robbed of your life energy by using the method offered in chapter 3 to diagnose and strengthen your aura.

People Who are Regularly Exposed to Energy Vampires in Their Personal or Professional Lives

Although sensitive people can feel the aggression emanating from energy thieves much more clearly than others, every individual suffers from being attacked by an energy vampire and from the atmospheric pollution that such an attack brings with it. Ignorance does not offer protection. On the contrary, when near an energy vampire, anyone whose aura has been weakened needs to be prepared, since the energy vampire's attacks can seriously harm the psyche. Sudden feelings of guilt, anxiety attacks, even overwhelming feelings of inferiority hit not only the victims of an attack but also outsiders who happen to be too close to such a scene.

People with Elevated Spiritual Consciousness, Healers, and Helpers

Those who have recently learned to open themselves spiritually are often the preferred victims for energy vampires. Those who know how to open their chakras (hidden energy centers) with the help of meditation exercises should also learn how to consciously close them again. Otherwise, they will be in constant danger of attack by energy vampires.

People who have jobs helping others are especially at risk of being attacked by energy vampires. These individuals are confronted day in and day out with their patients' psychological needs, problems, and damage (many of their patients are likely to suffer from problems, consciously or subconsciously, caused by the acts of energy vampires). Energy vampires find the doors open wider with these people than with most others. That is why professional healers and helpers need effective protection, to be able to open and cleanse themselves spiritually, but also to close themselves again.

In addition to strengthening your aura by using the exercises described in part 1 of this book and creating a spiritual safe area (part 2), I always recommend one more thing to my clients. Too many people have a tendency to abuse their subconscious, treating it as a kind of junkyard where they store all their repressed memories and any weak spots that their conscious self might consider embarrassing or unacceptable. Often energy vampires—especially the power and fear vampires—will try to weaken our defenses by causing feelings of guilt within us. In this manner, they undermine our self-confidence while positioning themselves as powerful, as knowing the way. To be able to protect ourselves effectively against energy thieves, it is not only imperative that we strengthen our aura, care for it, and learn the spiritual techniques to close it when necessary—it is also important to cleanse our subconscious of the psychological "garbage" that potential energy thieves can use as a way to gain access to our subconscious (parts 2 and 3 of the book).

1 Calculating Your Energy Balance and Individual Danger Zones

On the following pages, you will find detailed checklists with which you can determine whether you suffer from a shortage of life energy and where your danger zones lie: at work, with friends, in the family, in your relationship, or at home.

Answer the following questions spontaneously, without thinking them over too much. Following the questions are some guides on how to evaluate your answers; read these only after you have answered all the questions.

CHECKLIST 1: PERSONAL WELL-BEING AND SELF-ASSESSMENT

Are you often tired for no particular reason?   **yes/no**

Do you suffer from any of the following: nightmares,
insomnia, anxiety attacks, depression, lack of
motivation, concentration difficulties,
headaches, and/or dizziness?   **yes/no**

Are you often angry or worried about your
lack of vitality?   **yes/no**

Do you think you don't have enough money or
are not paid enough for your work?   **yes/no**

Do you often feel intimidated or crowded by the
physical and/or psychological presence of
another person?   **yes/no**

When you are with other people, do you often
feel stupid or clumsy, ugly, or weak?   **yes/no**

Do you frequently find it hard to concentrate
when you are near others, that you lose your
train of thought or have a hard time finding
the right words?   **yes/no**

Do you think you have more accidents or
mishaps than other people? Do you consider
yourself to be an unlucky person?   **yes/no**

Are you a victim of theft or robbery more frequently
than your neighbors or acquaintances?   **yes/no**

CHECKLIST 2: WORKPLACE AND JOB

Do you often dislike your job or where you
are in your career?   **yes/no**

Does the thought of going back to work after
a weekend or vacation depress you?   **yes/no**

Is there a tense atmosphere at your place of work?   **yes/no**

Is your company or department characterized by
    a strict hierarchy or set structure?   **yes/no**

Do your colleagues doubt your professional
    capacities?   **yes/no**

Do your colleagues sometimes treat you with
    a lack of respect?   **yes/no**

Are you under the impression that your workload
    does not match your talents and interests?   **yes/no**

When you think about work in the mornings,
    do you feel tired, grumpy, or discouraged?   **yes/no**

Do you feel exhausted after coming home from
    work at night?   **yes/no**

If you occasionally suffer from nightmares, do
    people or situations from work play a negative
    role in these dreams?   **yes/no**

If you own your company or are responsible for
    managing a business, do you have problems
    with low morale among employees, with excessive
    absences, theft, or bad feelings among employees?   **yes/no**

If you own a company or are responsible for
    managing a business, do you suffer from your
    competitors because of harsh competition or their
    superior implementation of ideas?   **yes/no**

CHECKLIST 3: CIRCLE OF FRIENDS

When you think of your friends, do you question
    whether they like you?   **yes/no**

After spending an evening or weekend with your
    friends, do you feel insecure or depressed?   **yes/no**

Do your friends frequently not respect your
convictions and try to convince you of their
opinions?   **yes/no**

In the presence of a friend, do you frequently get
the impression that he or she is "suffocating" you?   **yes/no**

Do some of your friends frequently ask for
admiration or other kinds of one-sided affection
from you?   **yes/no**

If you occasionally suffer from nightmares, do
your friends or does any one of your friends appear
in these dreams in a negative role?   **yes/no**

CHECKLIST 4: FAMILY AND RELATIONSHIPS

Do you often think or feel that you are not or
no longer happy with your spouse?   **yes/no**

When you think about your spouse, do you
spontaneously feel emotions like insecurity,
fear, or inadequacy?   **yes/no**

After having spent some intensive time with
your spouse, do you feel exhausted or empty?   **yes/no**

Does your spouse frequently ask for one-sided
affection from you, for example, because of
frequent illnesses or other reasons?   **yes/no**

Do you think you contribute more money,
ideas, and initiative of all sorts to your
relationship than your spouse?   **yes/no**

Do members of your family lose things or are
they robbed more frequently than neighbors or
friends? Has your house been broken into
or your car stolen?   **yes/no**

If You Have Children:

When thinking about your children (or one
of your children), do you suddenly feel insecure,
exhausted, or inadequate?   **yes/no**

Do you think you are unable to educate your
children (or one of your children) or have
failed as a parent?   **yes/no**

Are your children (or one of your children)
victims of accidents and mishaps more often
than others?   **yes/no**

Are your children (or one of your children)
frequently picked on by peers, made fun of,
or not taken seriously?   **yes/no**

If you have occasional nightmares, do family
members or scenes from your family life play
a negative role in these dreams?   **yes/no**

CHECKLIST 5: LEISURE TIME

Do you sometimes have to gather courage to
step outside the door?   **yes/no**

Do you believe that these days you are no longer
safe outside your own door?   **yes/no**

Do you sometimes have the feeling that someone
is following you?   **yes/no**

Have you ever been robbed or physically hurt
on a street or in a park?   **yes/no**

Are you frequently approached by religious sects,
pollsters, or other invasive people on the street?   **yes/no**

Do salespeople frequently try to talk you into the
purchase of a product rather than giving you
time to choose?   **yes/no**

Are such salespeople able to talk you into buying
products? yes/no
In cafés, subways, or other public places,
do you frequently have the feeling that other
people are staring at you? yes/no
Do you often have the feeling that strangers are
making fun of you, or are disrespectful
toward you? yes/no
After visiting public places or institutions—for
example, after a shopping trip or seeing a movie
or a play—do you frequently feel exhausted? yes/no

EVALUATING THE CHECKLISTS

To evaluate your energy level and identify your personal
danger zones, count your "yes" answers in the following
steps:

**Step A: Count how many times you answered "yes" in all
checklists combined:** _____

**Step B: Count how many times you answered "yes" in
each individual checklist:**

> ❯ Checklist 1: Personal Well-Being and
> Self-Assessment _____
> ❯ Checklist 2: Workplace and Job _____
> ❯ Checklist 3: Circle of Friends _____
> ❯ Checklist 4: Family and Relationships _____
> ❯ Checklist 5: Leisure Time _____

Once you have counted your "yes" answers, see the
descriptions below to evaluate your overall energy level based
on your answer to step A, the total amount of times you
answered "yes" in all of the checklists combined.

Not a Single "Yes"

Congratulations. If you did not answer a single question with "yes" in any of these checklists your personal energy level—and most likely also that of your spouse and family—is at the highest possible level. You seem to have more than enough energy, and there seems to be no vampire anywhere near you trying to latch on to your resources. The exercises presented in this book will assist you in generating energy to maintain this wonderful state.

One to Five "Yes" Answers

You suffer from a slight, or latent, lack of energy that you might hardly notice. But beware: what may start off small can quickly grow to larger losses. Consult the individual checklist analysis section to find out where your personal danger zones lie.

Six to Fifteen "Yes" Answers

You have an energy deficit that, while not acutely dangerous, is nonetheless significant enough not to have escaped your attention. Perhaps you have tried to hide this deficit from yourself and others, but you should stop such efforts immediately. Over the short and long term, you are in danger of suffering psychological or physical symptoms of fatigue, which you can effectively prevent now. Begin by reading the following individual checklist analysis section to find out where your personal danger zones lie.

Sixteen to Forty "Yes" Answers

You have a significant negative energy balance. You are probably aware that you need to do something to address your lack of vitality. Under no circumstances should you hesitate to reverse this negative trend. Read below for the analysis of your individual checklists to find out where to start your revitalization program.

Forty-one to Fifty "Yes" Answers

You have a dramatically negative energy balance! If you answered "yes" to this many questions, I would suggest seeking professional help immediately.

ANALYZING YOUR INDIVIDUAL CHECKLISTS

Now that you have identified your general energy level, look at your answers to step B—the amount of times you answered "yes" on each of the individual checklists. These numbers will help you identify your personal danger zones, the areas in which you are most vulnerable to an energy vampire attack.

In most cases, the individual analysis is quick and straightforward: Did you answer "yes" to questions significantly more often in one or two of the five checklists? If so, this is where your individual danger zones lie. Suppose you answered "yes" eleven times, with six of those responses in the second checklist, Workplace and Job. This indicates that you suffer from a considerable energy deficit caused predominantly by a person or circumstances in your professional life. Such circumstances can include power struggles and conspiracies among your colleagues (including bullying), but also general dissatisfaction with your job, position, or salary. To find out more about these types of problems, pay special attention to the third part of this book, "Protection against Energy Vampires in Business and the Workplace."

Another example might be if you answered "yes" thirteen times, with five "yes" answers in checklist 1, Personal Well-Being and Self-Assessment, and five "yes" answers in checklist 4, Family and Relationships. This means you suffer from a significant energy deficit caused primarily by negative energy inside you, which manifests itself most clearly in people and circumstances in your personal life—that is, in your relationships and family. To find out more about these types of problems, pay special attention to chapters 6, 13, and 14.

To better understand the individual checklist analysis, I recommend first reading parts 1 and 2 of this book. There, you will find many hints and examples that apply to and are significant for your personal situation and energy balance.

PART ONE

The Invisible Guard

i n this part of the book, we want to get to know our aura and experience its protective powers. We will find and fix any weak spots in our energy shield, cleanse and strengthen our aura, and take measures for its future care. After all, energy vampires are repelled by a strong aura.

By now, the importance of keeping the body healthy is fairly common knowledge. We try to eat things that have not been treated with excessive chemicals, consume lots of vegetables, and forgo toxins such as alcohol, nicotine, or other drugs. This is the only way that our organism can create the energy that we will need for our physical survival and our physical and spiritual well-being.

Looking after our physical health, however, is not enough. Our physical body is only the material aspect of ourselves, visible to everyone. In a way, it is the nucleus of our overall self, which, in large part, is composed of fine energy bodies. That is why it is necessary that we extend our physically healthy way of life to encompass precautions to care for and strengthen our energy components. We have to come to see caring for our aura as essential as caring for our skin, hair, muscles, and joints. Progressive people in the twenty-first century will be as conscious of their auras as we are now of our body and health.

2
Learn
to See Auras

even today there are those who have a clear sense of other peoples' auras. They can see or sense clearly if an aura is fit or has been neglected, whether it shines in energetic freshness, or lacks luster and shine like the fur of a sick animal. Because many of these aura-aware people are potential energy thieves, it is of special importance that we also are aware of our aura and that we can rely on the effectiveness of our protective energy mantel. If an energy vampire senses or sees that our aura is weak, or even has holes in it, he or she will not hesitate to attack. Conversely, we will feel much stronger if we have a strong aura and are aware of it. That is because a strong aura gets us in touch with a higher self that is spiritually much stronger and wiser than our smaller self. With the help of our higher self, we can face pretty much any danger.

STRUCTURE AND FUNCTIONING OF THE AURA

By now it is widely known that the aura can be made visible with technology—using high-frequency, so-called Kirlian photography (see figure 1).

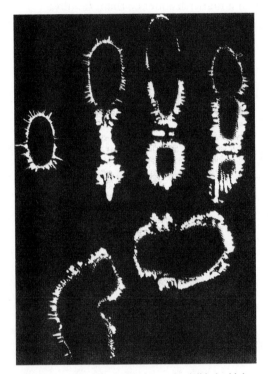

Figure 1. An aura of a handprint made visible by high-frequency Kirlian photography

Nonetheless, the various esoteric streams are not all unified in our aura. One usually differentiates between material, emotional, mental, and spiritual dimensions, which vibrate in different frequencies and influence each other (see figure 2 on page 24).

The Material Dimension

Let's start with the material dimension, which is easiest to grasp for most people. The material dimension is our physical body. Often people do not even count this dimension as part of our aura. After all, the aura is composed of energy, while our physical body consists of tangible matter. However, as modern science has shown, matter is nothing but compressed energy.

The material dimension is differentiated from the finer energy dimensions by its lower energy-wave frequency. Even though our bodies—like all animate and inanimate objects—are not static, the matter that makes up our bodies vibrates so slowly that it creates the impression of compact steadiness to our senses.

The Mental Dimension

Just as we can describe our physical body as compressed energy fields, the seemingly invisible higher dimensions of our aura can be defined as tangible matter. In this sense, we can speak of a mental aura dimension, or a mental body. This dimension resides in a higher frequency than the physical body, but in a lower frequency than the emotional (or astral) and spiritual dimensions. The mental level is the dimension of consciousness; it is home to our intellect, our conscious thoughts, and our ideas.

The Emotional or Astral Dimension

The next-highest frequency level of our aura is the emotional dimension, which is also referred to as the astral dimension. Emotions and the subconscious show up in the light of our aura on a noticeably higher level than the mental sphere (contrary to what some Western psychologists might expect). They belong to the astral level, which most people access only through the dream state. It is possible to use more involved creative processes, such as trances and other types of meditation, to gain conscious access to the astral level. But since the astral dimension is not usually in contact with our consciousness, it is much more vulnerable to psychic attacks than is the mental level.

Most of us will, at least once in our lives, have the sensation of *feeling* (not seeing) someone looking at us—in a large crowd, for example—or of *feeling* (not hearing) someone following us. These extrasensory warning signals are sent by our aura, and can also be visualized as a preemptive "energy boundary" of our psyches.

Just as we feel an invasion of our personal space when someone gets too close to us, we can feel an invasion of our much larger individual aura space: as soon as someone or something enters this energy space, our aura alarm system is activated. Thus, at its core, psychic self-defense is rather basic: you simply have to learn to pick up on the senses and alarm messages of your aura and consciously redirect them.

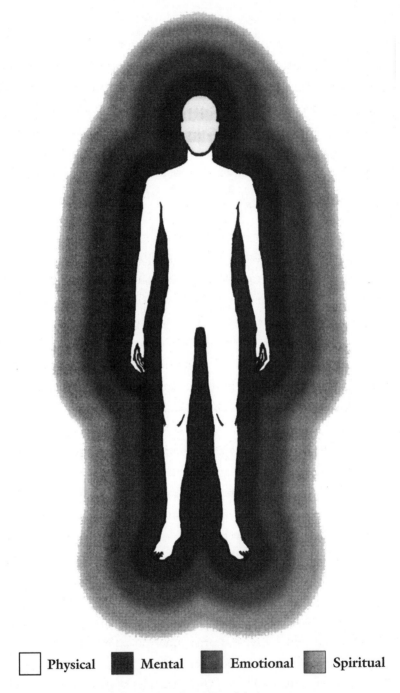

▢ Physical   ■ Mental   ■ Emotional   ■ Spiritual

Figure 2. The four dimensions of the human aura

The Spiritual Dimension

It is only through the aura that one can gain access to the higher self, which resides on the spiritual level and has the highest energy frequency. Getting in contact with our higher self allows us to get in touch with cosmic wisdom and our eternal soul, that ever-present spark of energy from which all life originated. Although people in times past were able to get in touch with their spiritual selves through mystical meditation, this ability eludes the majority of people today. Using the meditation and visualization exercises in this book, I wish to awaken this valuable ability in my readers.

THE COLORS OF OUR AURA

With some practice, most people are able not only to see their own aura and those of others, but also to assess health and emotional states by the color, shine, and expansion of the aura. Most often, it is the emotional aura level that is visible to our physical eye: with healthy people it usually sparkles and shines in strong shades of green, yellow, blue, or red.

It is impossible to objectively define the meaning of each of these colors, in part because they depend on the subjective perception of the beholder, or the person emitting the aura. But there are some experiences regarding the meaning of the colors that, in large part, form the basis for aura diagnosis.

For example, as a rule of thumb, we can say that red signifies a strong will, as well as a tendency for a quick temper. However, if this color in your aura means something else to you, you are probably correct in your feeling. It is, after all, your aura, and nobody knows it better than you.

GREEN: Green is the color of health, of natural growth, and of groundedness.

RED AND ORANGE: Red and orange signify a strong will and perseverance, but also a bad temper.

BLUE: A predominance of blue shades signifies a calm nature, the ability to communicate, and spiritual wisdom. However, it often also indicates a latent lack of determination and vitality.

YELLOW: Dominating shades of yellow signal a strong mental level of reason and consciousness.

PINK: Pink suggests healing powers, but also a certain indecisiveness.

PURPLE: Purple stands for spiritual security and psychic abilities.

BROWN: Shades of brown indicate a close connection with the earth, but can also signify deep connection with the past and a potentially underdeveloped ego.

WHITE: White is the color of cleansing, liberation, and purity. It is the color of security and leadership and grows out of the presence of the higher self.

BLACK AND GRAY: Shades of black and gray indicate illness, energy blockades. If black is clearly predominant, it also means impending death. Gray aura spots can be left by energy vampires. Gray aura spots signal that that person's aura is weakened and energetically polluted. Thus, people with partially gray auras may have been the victims of energy vampires—or may become the latest prey of thieves looking for a new victim. Often, one person fits both categories.

The ability to see the auras of living beings is often misleadingly characterized as a psychic ability; however, it does not necessarily require extrasensory abilities. While there are people who see the fine-substance components of living beings through the third eye,* there are many others—including myself—who simply use the physical sense of sight to recognize and "read" auras.

There are also many people who are less visually oriented and are thus not able to see auras with their eyes, even after performing the focusing exercises. You shouldn't worry if you are part of this group: there are other ways to recognize auras.

Many people who have not been able to see auras since their child-

---

*The third eye is a chakra point that is most commonly thought to be located in the space between the two eyebrows (see figure 4 on page 67).

hood or who have no conscious recollection of ever having seen auras regain this ability, even without the use of exercises, at a totally unexpected moment. For example, many survivors of catastrophes and accidents report that the people around them who were involved in those dramatic scenes of life and death appeared to "duplicate" themselves, such as in the following short case studies:

- In stormy waters, a person was blown off the deck of a ship. Even while he was falling, his aura emerged as a shining coat of light around the contour of his body.
- A survivor of a car accident was trapped in the wrecked car and saw how the body of the driver next to him seemed to double and was "shining in brilliant colors." He said the pulsating aura emerged from the bent body of the injured man and seemed to envelop him like a warm cloak. Doctors afterward called it a miracle that the man, despite his severe, open wounds, did not bleed to death.

I also know many people who can emotionally "scan" auras. Others are able to recognize the appearance and consistency of auras by touch. And there are those who are particularly sensitive and can recognize auras through extrasensory perception in their third eye.

If, after performing the exercises that follow, you are not (or not yet) able to see auras, ask yourself this: What is my strongest sense? Then try to sense auras with that sense, be it a sense of touch, intuition, or anything else.

One more tip: For the exercises described throughout the book, it is not necessary for you to see your own aura or those of others. The exercises depend much more on visualizing auras, chakras, and other energy phenomenon, to imagine them with your spiritual eye. Experience shows that these visualization exercises are also effective in activating your ability to *see* auras.

PRELIMINARY EXERCISE: AN INSTANT WAY TO FEEL THE AURA

The simplest way to experience an aura is to briefly and forcefully rub your hands against one another for a minute and then separate your two palms slightly, leaving a distance of only about one centimeter between them. Notice the electric static, the weak but noticeable resistance that is a result of the colliding of two energy fields.

EXERCISE 1: FINGER GAMES

The human eye contains parts known as rods, which are located primarily on the edges of our field of vision. These receptors are activated in weak light through a biochemical process during which they synthesize the substance rhodopsin. We usually need these rods in order to see in darkness; moreover, they enable us to see things in the periphery of our field of vision. In brighter light, the rhodopsin quickly fades. But if we focus our eyes on the edge of our field of vision in dim light—the famous cross-eyed look depicted in so many illustrations of visionaries and holy people—we can, with some experience, see the auras that surround every living being.

In the following exercise, be sure to avoid straining your eyes. When your eyes are strained what you see may at first resemble an aura but is often just a deceptive after-image, a visual negative, of the physical person. Below are some helpful rules of thumb to differentiate the after-image from an aura:

➐ The aura is composed of translucent, fluorescent colors. The after-image is usually monochrome.

❯ The aura is a fluid energy field that moves by itself. The after-image is like a shadow of the moving body: if the body remains still, so does the after-image.

❯ The aura can exhibit different colors. The after-image is always the negative of the object. For example, if a person wears a white shirt, that person's after-image will have a black torso; if the person has red hair, the after-image seems to have a green light on its head, and so forth.

Finding a Place for the Exercise

Sit down in a comfortable position in a place where you will not be disturbed. If this place is outside, go at dawn or sunset. If you are in an enclosed space, make sure the lights are dimmed. There should be neither an artificial light source nor rays of sunlight in your direct field of vision. You'll need to face a wall or a similar surface area: this projection area should be in muted, dark colors, perhaps a brown wall or a dark green forest. There should be no objects between you and the surface on which you will focus.

Relaxation and Internal Preparation

Close your eyes halfway and relax by visualizing pictures that create pleasant feelings within you. After several minutes of relaxation, open your eyes again. Your eye muscles should now be as relaxed as your spirit.

The Exercise

Spread the fingers of both your hands at eye level and slowly move your hands toward one another as if you were about to fold them. Form an imaginary ball in your hands while keeping a distance of about one half inch between the

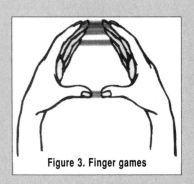

Figure 3. Finger games

opposite fingers of both hands (see figure 3).

Now focus your eyes—in as relaxed a manner as possible—on the empty space between your fingers. Look into this "alley" made by the tips of your index, middle, ring, and pinky fingers for about a minute, with your distant focus projected into the center of this alley.

After a few minutes, you will probably see something resembling thin smoke or steam clouds, fine threads of energy in a lustrous fog, which connect the tips of your fingers with one another.

Variation and Repetition

If you are not at first successful with this exercise, remain relaxed and confident. Try it again in a different place—in a room instead of outside, or vice versa—or at a different time of day, when you are more relaxed. In any case, you should interrupt this exercise after a few minutes of focusing and wait at least five minutes before starting again, to avoid overexerting your eye muscles, which will only lead you to see the "pseudo-aura," the after-image previously described.

REMINDER: With all of the exercises throughout this book, it is important to remember not to give up if you fail at first. Seeing auras is literally child's play, which means that as adults we may need to try a few times before we get the hang of it. It also means that it is more than likely that you, too, will be successful with the exercises eventually.

EXERCISE 2: SEEING A PARTNER'S AURA

Again, choose a place—inside or outside—where you will not be disturbed. Ask your partner (someone you trust without reservations) to do the following exercise with you. Just as in the previous exercise, you should dim the lights.

Ask your partner to stand about three feet away from the projection area (e.g., a dark wall), facing you. Position yourself about ten feet away from your partner and look at him or her.

Be careful not to stare as you look at your partner with a relaxed gaze and make use of your peripheral vision, where most of the rods are located. Don't look straight at your partner; just glance at him or her before focusing on his or her contour—the outline of his or her shoulder or temple, for example.

Stop this exercise after about a minute and rest your eyes for at least five minutes before starting again. During these breaks, sit still with your eyes half closed.

A Ring of Rays

After you have repeated this exercise two or three times, you will probably see lustrous clouds of steam or fog that seem to be emerging from the shoulder or temple of your partner. If you are not successful even after repeated attempts (remember to rest!), try the following exercises, which, in my experience, can be very successful.

EXERCISE 3: MUSICAL AURA STIMULATION

There is hardly a stimulant stronger for the human aura—as well as that of plants and animals—than music. The kind of music that will arouse the aura of your partner depends on individual taste. However, certain modern variations of pop music, especially aggressive types of techno and heavy metal, are at odds with the frequency of our auras.

Preparation

Retreat with your partner to a place where you will not be disturbed. Turn on music that your partner has chosen for the occasion. You can play the music over speakers, or ask your partner to listen to it with headphones. Again, the lights should be dimmed.

Ask your partner to stand about three feet from the projection area (e.g., a dark wall), facing you. Position yourself about thirteen feet away from your partner and look at him or her with a relaxed gaze. Make use of your peripheral vision. Don't stare at your partner; just glance at his or her contour—the outline of his or her shoulder or temple, for example.

Dancing Rays

Stop this exercise after about a minute and allow your eyes to rest for at least five minutes before beginning anew. Remain seated during these breaks with your eyes half closed. After you have repeated this exercise two or three times, you should see lustrous clouds of steam or fog that seem to emerge from the shoulder or temple of your partner. They will be moving in rhythm to the music and change colors depending on the pitch of the melody. The aura should be more visible than in the previous exercise without music.

Variation and Repetition

If you have experienced only minimal or no success with these exercises, stay relaxed and confident. If your partner in these exercises is a person that you trust completely (and vice versa) you might consider asking him or her to take part in the following variation of the exercise. At this point, however, it might make sense to change roles regularly so that you and your partner take turns being the beholder (or "watcher") and the watched.

EXERCISE 4: DRESS OF RAYS

Nothing blocks the clear visibility of the human aura more than the clothes we wear. Any kind of clothing makes the visual perception of auras much more difficult. The human eye, even after substantial practice, is limited in its ability to differentiate between the colors of the aura and those of the clothing. Those individuals who have no, or only little, experience in seeing auras might thus perceive only a vague circle of colors where the energy colors of the aura mix with the more mundane colors of a shirt and pants, or a blouse and skirt.

Because even the colors black and white interact with the colors of the aura, I recommend this fourth exercise to all those who, even after repeating the first through third exercises, were unsuccessful in seeing the aura.

If the nature of the relationship between you and your partner makes it possible, you may have better success if you repeat the second and/or third exercise in the nude.

This variation is not recommended for (or acceptable to) everybody, especially since it might be harder with little or no clothing to concentrate with the necessary degree of relaxation. It is certainly not necessary to perform the exercise without any clothing—for example, you could concentrate on perceiving the part of the aura that surrounds your or your partner's torso.

However, if you are not distracted by this variation, you should be able, after some repetitions (remember to rest!), to see the musically stimulated and uninhibited aura of your partner. You will probably see it as a colored cloud of fog, as a pulsating energy field along the part of the body outline on which you are focusing.

3
Strengthening Your Aura

j ust as people differ in their physical appearance, each individual has a unique aura. Neither the interaction of the colors nor the outline and expansion of an aura is the same for any two people. Many people are surrounded by an aura as tight and smooth as a second, shining skin. With others, it often expands three feet or more past the physical outline of their body. The expansion of the aura certainly depends on whether we have a high or a low energy level and whether we are oriented toward the inside or the outside—whether we are an introverted dreamer or artist or an extroverted socialite and activist.

Have you ever wondered why some people are constantly harassed by salespeople, pollsters, and religious cults, while others are never the targets of such invasive people? By now, the answer is probably clear to you: those who have strengthened their auras and are conscious of the exchange of energy are able to deter those who would waste time, invade personal space, and feed off of the energy of others.

With some practice, it is possible to tell a person's character and condition by the predominant colors of his or her aura. For example, people with a predominantly blue aura are usually pragmatic and less vivacious. For people of this type, the aura is generally not expanded far beyond their physical outlines. On the other hand, individuals whose auras are dominated by red, orange, and magenta colors tend to be ambitious but also ill-tempered—their auras will often extend far beyond their bodies.

Color diagnosis can be difficult due to the numerous variables behind the significance of each color (as discussed in chapter 2). Yet it is universally accepted that when the observed person has an aura with gray or black spots, immediate intervention is necessary. These colors can indicate extremely dangerous leaks through which life energy (even without outside provocation) can leave the body. At the very least, they indicate hardened spots (which, in this context, I refer to as aura scars) where the circulation of energy is blocked.

The stronger our aura, the more effective it is in protecting us from energy vampires. Just as a good physical immune system can be the best defense against viruses in our midst, an intact and "in shape" aura can offer the best defense against an unhealthy psychic atmosphere. The unhealthy atmospheres frequently found in large offices, for example, don't just pollute with electronic noise, chemical products, bad lighting, and the like—they often contain the excessive psychic pollution of bullying colleagues and overly ambitious superiors.

The exercises described in this chapter are designed to strengthen your aura. Whether you experience a weak, spotted aura or simply wish to boost your aura immune system to cleanse and protect yourself from external factors, the following exercises will allow you to enjoy greater confidence and higher self-esteem. If you follow these visualizations on a regular basis, energy vampires will no longer be able to suck up your life energies.

Have you ever heard the stories of the "holy people of the pillars," which were told to some of us during our religious instruction? The stories spoke of holy people who, in the times of the Old Testament, would stay up on high pillars for days, weeks, and even months on end to prove their love for the gods.

Even back then, as a young girl ten or twelve years old, I thought that something was not quite right about this story: Why should these holy people climb pillars and stay on top of them for extended periods of time? The explanation offered to me ("because of their obedience") was not convincing—it was not until many years later that I came upon a meaning that seemed to make more sense.

CASE STUDY: HOLY PEOPLE OF THE PILLARS

A while back I had a client, Monica M., who had consulted me as a spiritual energy and life consultant. She was a young, attractive woman in her late twenties in a difficult personal situation. She was about to separate from her boyfriend, who was no longer willing to accompany her on her spiritual path of growth (sometimes we have to leave people behind who are obstacles in our development). However, he did not want to accept her decision and pressured her incessantly, sometimes with threats, to return to him.

When she visited my practice for the first time, Monica was somewhat scared and confused. We first performed some exercises to strengthen her aura (though not the pillar-of-light exercise, which became part of my program as a result of my experience with Monica). The first consultation was rather turbulent. The distressed client broke into tears on several occasions and, during the session, her boyfriend was at my door and demanded that my assistant allow him to speak with Monica. Even though my assistant (who had received energy training) quickly sent the man off, his loud voice was audible in the room, where it further upset my client.

The night after this turbulent session, I dreamed that Monica was once again being chased by her boyfriend. Scared, she fled from him across a kind of field of ruins and rocks—which I recognized to be ruins from the times of the Old Testament. Weathered pillars stood all around her. However, there was one pillar in particular, just steps away from the fleeing woman, that was different than the others.

The pillar was glowing in a bright light. Unlike the others, it seemed not to be made out of stone. Rather, it was constructed out of pure light. Monica touched the pillar with both her hands and the light parted and let her inside. Now she was inside the glowing pillar, visible as if behind glass and lit up by bright lights. But when her boyfriend tried to follow her, the glass repelled him as though it were bulletproof.

In the dream, Monica was smiling. And while she was smiling, she was lifted up in this pillar of light; she slowly floated upward until she ended up on top of the shining pillar. "A holy person of the pillar!" I thought— and woke up at that moment.

I had my dream diary next to my bed as always—there is further discussion on the help a diary can provide in chapter 6—so I was able to write down this impressive dream right away and capture the explanation of the myth of the "holy people of the pillars" that it offered. From this dream sprang the following exercise for the strengthening of the aura, which I now use for myself and for my clients. After all, what else could this pillar of light have been but a beautiful, precise visualization of our aura, which protects and envelops us, but at the same time connects us with our higher self (thus the lifting up on top of the pillar)?

A few weeks after our first session, Monica M. had strengthened her aura and self-confidence (receiving help from the new pillar-of-light exercise) so that she was able to convince her former partner of the harm and futility of his deeds. After she had explained her reasons and decision to him in a calm voice and with carefully chosen words, he was visibly impressed and taken aback. He wished her all the best for her future and tearfully said a final goodbye.

EXERCISE 1: THE PILLAR OF LIGHT

Go to a quiet place where you will not be disturbed. Dim the lights and eliminate all sources of noise. Sit or lie down and get comfortable, close your eyes and breathe in and out regularly until you can feel your body relaxing and your attention turning to your inside world.

Now imagine that you see a place with your third eye— the chakra from which you receive a spiritual sense of vision (see figure 4, page 67)—and this place is the very definition of safe and peaceful for you.

What kind of place is this? It is different for every person. For some, it is a clearing in a forest, while for others it is a green mountain pasture. Or perhaps you are envisioning a chapel, a cavern, or a small park? Take the time to find your precise place. Imagine it thoroughly, until you can see it clearly with your spiritual eye. Then visualize yourself entering this place. Experience how good you feel there. Feel the mild air on your skin, the ground beneath you, take in the wonderful scent of this place.

Whatever this place of yours looks like, after some time you will recognize that there is an axis in its center—a pillar that rises up from the center of your place and goes up into the sky. This axis is the center of your self, your internal life that roots you in the earth and at the same time connects you with the heaven of spirituality high above you. Take a good look at this axis: it is thicker than a one-hundred-year-old oak tree; it seems incredibly solid and trustworthy. Your sky-reaching "tree of life" is lit up like a thick ray of sunlight; it seems to be as massive as ancient wood and yet is made up of sheer energy, of white light that pulsates slowly but strongly.

Inside the Pillar of Light

Now step inside this pillar of light. Be conscious of how you enter the vertical light shaft and how the rays gently start going through your body. Spread your arms, and let the light enter you.

Feel the rays massage your aura, hear the static as they mix, and feel your aura become as brilliant as the light of this pillar.

Watch your aura moving fluidly, how every single color in your energy coat is becoming brighter, shinier, and more expressive.

Feel your aura expand. Feel its circumference and its out-line (with either your physical or your spiritual hands). You will come to realize that your aura is oval—the shape of an egg, the source of all life.

Check Your Aura for Holes and Scars

Now slowly run your hands along your aura. Support this exercise with your spiritual eye: do you notice spots where energy flows less freely or is blocked, or is there a gray or black spot on your aura? Examine these spots with particular care and massage your aura until these spots shine in bright colors.

Groom Your Aura

Now straighten and groom your aura with your fingers spread wide. Imagine it consisting of threads of energy, of a web of pure light that covers you from head to toe. Carefully pull this web apart, find out how much you can stretch the web, and shape it into the form that pleases you the most. Be conscious that your aura gains vitality, energy, and shine with every touch—either from the pillar of light or from your hands.

Affirmation

Repeat to yourself several times:

> *"I am ready for any psychological*
> *attack—only positive energies can*
> *penetrate my shield."*

Repeat this affirmation to yourself until you are completely sure that this protective energy will be a reliable guard. If you feel the need to guard yourself further, observe the outside area of your aura and watch as the clear area slowly starts to crystallize—like water that is slowly freezing into ice. Your aura is just as transparent as before, but no one can penetrate it any longer without your permission: you are inside an indestructible oval of crystal lights.

Meeting Your Higher Self

Encased in your egg-shaped aura, you are still inside your tree of life and energy—your pillar of light. You should not leave this pillar of light without having contacted your higher self.

Consciously rise up slowly inside your pillar of light. The energy axis in the center of your self roots you with the material world while also connecting you with the spiritual level of your existence. Feel how you continue floating upward in your axis of light until you have arrived at the top. Experience the feeling of merging with your higher self for a moment: like a holy person of the pillar, you are now sitting on top of the pillar of light, with your legs crossed, looking down at your happy place. Observe how beautiful this place is, how it is illuminated by the light.

Humbly, think about how much more powerful and wise the higher self is than the smaller I, which is the only "I" you are usually aware of. This higher self is your connection to the wisdom of creation, to God, or to whatever else you choose to call this cosmic force. Through your higher self you are part of a universal energy, and as long as you are in touch with it, you have infinite energy reserves and are able to accomplish extraordinary things—and experience extraordinary insights.

Slowly separate yourself from your higher self and feel yourself gliding back down to the ground inside your pillar of light.

Ending the Exercise

Once you have reached the bottom of your axis of light, make sure that your aura is intact, shining, and surrounding you while pulsating with energy. You are safe. You have felt the presence and wisdom of your higher self. You are sparkling with energy. No being or situation can steal your energy.

With this in mind, step out of your pillar of light, cross back through to your happy place, and slowly return to the external world. Open your eyes. Do you see your aura? It is shining and tingling; from now on it will forever cover you as an indestructible cover of pulsating light.

Repetitions

For the first couple of weeks, I recommend repeating this exercise once a day. Later on, it may suffice to enter your pillar of light and make contact with your higher self on a weekly or even monthly basis. And one day, you may feel that the consciousness of an intact aura never leaves you— not while awake, nor when sleeping.

Just as we wash dust and dirt off our hair and skin after a long day or upon returning from a trip, we need to cleanse our aura on a regular basis. After all, it is an energy filter that shields us from countless particles of atmospheric pollution. On days when it has to suffer through stress, fights, and smog, the aura of most people is literally spiked with negative energy particles.

Those who are able to read your aura can tell you flat out, even after a glance, what sorts of obstacles you had to overcome that day—such as a bombardment of electrical "smog" at the office or a hail of bad wishes from envious colleagues after the meeting at which your promotion was announced. Because of what has occurred during especially turbulent days, at night our aura can be just as gray with exhaustion and pollution as our skin. That pollution hinders the flow of energy and can even completely block it at spots that are badly affected. This weakens our aura and facilitates the work of energy vampires. To allow our aura to recover entirely, we ought to cleanse it on a regular basis. This ensures that no negative thoughts or feelings we are bombarded with can get through.

EXERCISE 2: CLEANSING YOUR AURA OF DAILY ENERGY WASTE

To facilitate the visualization of cleansing your aura, I usually recommend performing this short exercise while taking a shower. While your aura cannot really be cleansed with water and soap, the visualization is helped as you imagine the energy particles rain down on you like warm water.

Preparation

For a few minutes, retreat to a warm place where you are sure you will not be disturbed (preferably in or close to the bathroom). Remind yourself that your aura is enveloping and protecting you as always. But also be aware that your aura is exhausted and tired after a long day. Continue thinking about this, and when you are ready, remove your clothing and get under the shower.

Shining Drops of Energy on Your Skin

Direct the water in a soft shower so that it hits your head at the location of your crown chakra (see figure 4 in chapter 5). Visualize the water as shining drops of energy that are about to cleanse the skin of your aura.

Feel how these drops of energy gently stick to the external side of your aura to cleanse and revitalize it. Feel the drops running down along the edge of your aura, taking impurities with it. Observe how the glowing drops of energy finally run down the drain on their way back to the cosmic origin of all energy, where they will be cleansed and recycled before returning to us.

While these drops are running along the skin of your aura, carefully examine this skin with your spiritual eye and your spiritual hands. Do you still see gray, black, hardened, or polluted spots? If so, massage them softly until every last impurity in your aura has been released and washed away.

Ending the Exercise and Repetition

When you are sure that your aura is entirely cleansed, finish your shower and dry yourself off until your skin feels as energetic as your revitalized aura did a minute ago.

In the beginning, repeat this exercise at least once a week. Later, once you have become more conscious of your aura, it will be enough to carry out this cleansing ritual whenever you feel that your aura has been polluted.

In any case, you should cleanse your aura before performing the exercise 3 on page 49.

As I mentioned in the introduction, energy vampires frequently use the material that people dump in the junkyard of their subconscious—suppressed desires or feelings of guilt. It is an unchangeable, cosmic law that we can only attract those events, people, or situations for which there exist parallels inside of us. Misfortunes that one experiences become personal "fate" if one does not deal with these "magnets of misfortune" in one's subconscious.

To illustrate this point I provide below two examples of typical situations that I have encountered in my work as a spiritual energy and lifestyle consultant.

CASE STUDY: A VICIOUS CYCLE OF ENERGIES

One day, a young man named Sean F. came to see me. He had an impressive knowledge of computer programming and vast professional experience. "But," he told me, "for some reason the technology directors at companies where I interview have the tendency of starting out by lauding me far past my achievements, only to exaggerate my weaknesses after just a few weeks or months. It is not long before I am back without a job, because I either gave up and resigned—or was fired."

Even while Sean was complaining to me about his misfortune, I could read his life story. His aura was dominated almost exclusively by subdued colors—a clear predominance of pastel blue, which at many spots appeared almost gray.

It is an unchangeable, cosmic law that we can only attract those events, people, or situations for which there exist parallels inside of us.

I told him straight to his face: "You expect an unfortunate development every time—and then you are surprised that your secret prophecy
is fulfilled?" It became increasingly clear during subsequent sessions that
Sean subtly suggested to each of his bosses that he would be unable to
fulfill the expectations they had of him—and that it would thus be best
to let him go.

"The crazy thing about that," continued Sean, "is that I—at least
initially—know for sure that I am able to meet all that is required of me
almost without effort. In the beginning, I am hardly able to temper my
excitement. But for some reason I suddenly fall into a black hole, my
boss starts criticizing my work, which indeed starts getting worse. And
then, there is often even some colleague around me who shines with
energy and ideas at my expense!"

"What do you mean, at your expense?" I asked him, becoming even
more attuned to his problem. Sean gave me a confused look. He wasn't
quite sure what he meant by that. But the more he thought about it, the
more he was able to verbalize the phenomenon.

"In almost every company where I have worked, there is a mild-man-
nered colleague that from day one starts observing me closely. At first, it
always seems like he will be the next one to be fired. That makes him all
the more devoted in his admiration for my energy. He appears in awe of
my presence, brilliant mind, and so on. And, after all, everyone likes this
kind of admiration—who would push such a person away?"

"But somehow," he continued, "this relationship starts reversing itself
over time: suddenly it is he who is full of energy and initiative, he who
solves the most difficult problems, and he who suddenly gets all the
compliments and bonuses from the boss of our section, who at the same
time starts to give me those critical looks. . . . In some bizarre manner,
what I feared from the beginning comes true again. But it is all the
stranger that this seemingly lackluster colleague and I switch roles in
such a short time!"

I diagnosed this as a clear case of an encounter with an energy vampire. With his weakened—and, at places, incomplete—aura, Sean was

unable to put up much resistance to the thieving attacks of his colleague (which may not even have been conscious ones). Because of this, his colleague would feast on Sean's energy. And because Sean, from the beginning, expected something like this to happen, those negative emotional and mental thoughts opened him wide for energy theft. A colleague who lacked life energy could intuitively feel this chance—and take advantage of it without hesitating.

CASE STUDY: STOLEN LOVE ENERGY

The second case study that I'll describe seems, in some aspects, to represent a fate typically associated with women. To prevent any misunderstanding, I define fate as events, circumstances, or people that we attract in the external world, which are based on certain configurations inside us. To put it differently: if we change the structures in our conscious or subconscious minds, we will change our fate, which will keep us away from misfortunes, illness, or worse. Fate is not something we are sent, but something that we create for ourselves.

Let us call the young woman Lola S. She was Latin American and very good looking, which led to many suitors, both older and younger. But what might have been a positive situation under different circumstances ended up becoming a problem for Lola. She worked as a waitress in a bar, and "for some dark reason," as she explained, "men show an alarming lack of respect in dealing with me!"

I could see that Lola was not the kind of woman whose dress, makeup, and body language would have suggested to men that she was looking for an adventure. Still, she alone kept receiving propositions from the male patrons of the bar, even though she worked alongside a number of other young women who were no less attractive and, in some cases, were considerably more free-spirited. It was not rare for her admirers to wait for her after her shift, to follow her home, to call to her on the street and try and get her attention, and so on. After she had twice been in situations where she—in her view—had barely avoided being sexually assaulted, she decided to seek my counsel.

In this case, too, it was not hard for me to recognize that the frequency of more-or-less violent, sexually motivated (verbal or physical) attacks had to be based on some sort of parallel construction in the subconscious of Lola S.

We were quickly able to dismiss the more obvious explanation that the young woman somehow "secretly wished" for the things that kept happening to her: Lola was in a fulfilling relationship, and, I might add, the idea of suppressed nymphomania in general seems to be more a male fantasy than fact.

What was a lot more plausible—and what turned out to be true—was the following explanation: Due to certain highly traumatic events in her childhood and early youth, Lola had learned to be prepared for constant sexual or sexually oriented transgressions. Because of this fear of once again becoming a victim, she kept attracting potential attackers—thus the surprising frequency of aggressive suitors around her. At the same time, these traumatic childhood experiences had never been properly processed by Lola and had left harsh marks on her aura: even during our first encounter, I noticed that the energy field of this young woman had an ugly, gray aura scar situated on her back at the level of her shoulder blades.

In both cases—for Sean F. and Lola S.—we were able to strengthen the weakened aura through an exercise program. We were able to close holes and to revitalize the energy field and harden it against attacks from the outside.

But, in both cases, it was equally important to stop energy vampires by preventing latent attacks from the inside as well. The simplest method to neutralize the negative energy effects of these "Trojan horses" inside us is to reprogram our consciousness using the aura-strengthening visualization exercises.

As I will explain in the remainder of this book, it is also necessary to cleanse our subconscious of all negative thoughts, feelings, and images; only by doing so can we ensure that energy vampires are not attracted by the emotional baggage we store in our psyches. However, as an immediate measure to strengthen our aura, it is useful to erect a spiritual barrier, even before cleansing our subconscious. This barrier will be impossible for external aggressors to overcome, even if they—as in the cases of Sean and Lola—are tempted by the magnets of misfortune inside us.

EXERCISE 3: STRENGTHEN YOUR AURA THROUGH CONSCIOUSNESS TRAINING

Go to a quiet place where you know you won't be disturbed. Dim the lights and turn off any sources of noise. Sit or lie down and make yourself comfortable. Close your eyes. Slowly and regularly, breathe in and out until you can feel your physical tension easing and your attention turning to the world inside you.

Focus your awareness on the strengthened and revitalized aura that surrounds you as a colorful field of pulsating energy. Using your spiritual eye, carefully look at your aura. Feel it with your spiritual hands: your aura is closely surrounding your body, like a well-tailored suit of pure light.

Now start breathing in and out more deeply and feel how your aura expands as you breathe in and contracts as you breathe out. Your aura is like a second skin that envelops you tightly, prickling with energy.

Feel how your aura expands further with each breath. As you exhale now, it no longer contracts but continues to inflate further, like a balloon you are blowing up.

Feel how the expansion of your aura is growing and see how its shape changes the farther away it moves from the contours of your body.

Continue breathing air into your aura until it has the shape of a large egg. You are once again inside an oval made up of white light.

Shield Your Aura by Programming Your Consciousness

Once again, run your spiritual hands along the surface of your aura. Feel how hard it is, a mental shield against the attacks of energy vampires. Get acquainted with the nature of this shield until you continue to feel its presence even after you stop touching it with your spiritual hands.

Repeat several times, either out loud or to yourself:

> *"I am shielded against any psychic attack.*
> *Only positive energy can penetrate*
> *my shield."*

Now recite this affirmation, either out loud or to yourself, in synchrony with your breathing. Repeat it seven or twelve times—these are frequencies proven to be the most responsive to the human subconscious. In this way, you instill in your consciousness the certainty that your shield will protect you, even against attacks that could be caused by any magnets of misfortune inside you.

Spikes of Light

Observe how this consciousness programming affects your aura. Sharp spikes emerge from the smooth surface of light. These spikes resemble those of a thorn bush or a porcupine that is preparing to defend itself against a predator. Your aura is forming shining spikes of light on its surface, spikes that extend outward in all directions. These spikes become ever more numerous, until the entire surface of your aura is covered with these shining spikes.

With your spiritual fingers, touch these spikes—carefully, so as to not hurt yourself.

Repeat several times, either out loud or to yourself:

"My shield will defeat anyone who attacks
me—even if my attacker was drawn
to me by negative thoughts inside me.
The spikes of my aura allow entry
only to positive energies."

Repeat this affirmation until you are fully aware of the protective spikes of light, even when you don't touch them with your spiritual fingers.

Now observe how the spikes retreat into the surface of your aura. Say the following out loud or to yourself:

"When I need these spikes, they will
be there immediately."

Feel and see how the surface of your aura once again becomes smooth and even.

Ending the Exercise, Repetition

Once you have become fully acquainted with your new aura defenses and their protective effects, focus again on your breathing. Turn your awareness to the fact that your aura is now once again contracting every time you exhale, until it once again wraps tightly around your body.

Open your eyes and slowly return to your external reality. Within the next couple of days, it is recommended that you occasionally check whether your aura will indeed extend its spikes when you want it to; this is simply a precaution. To be entirely sure, you should repeat this exercise once a week for the first couple of months. By then you will be thoroughly convinced that your aura protection will be there anytime you need it.

4 Emergency Measures for Immediate Psychic Defense

the more energy we are able to produce within us, the easier and more effective it will be for us to defend ourselves against attacks by energy vampires. That is why I always recommend regular spiritual and physical workouts—such as yoga and meditation—in order to build up spiritual energy. If our energy reserves are filled to the brim, we are able not only to deter any vampiric aggression but also to extend our spiritual defense shield to third parties, if needed. Those third parties could be our children or sick people under our care—those who would be unable to defend themselves without our immediate energy help.

AN ELITE MEANS OF DEFENSE:
FLOOD THE ATTACKER WITH ENERGY

I recommend the elite energy defense, which has worked since biblical times, only to "energy millionaires"—those who are more than able to control the flow of their energies. Have you ever tried to drown an attacker with your love?

CASE STUDY: AN AUTOMOBILE BREAKDOWN IN THE SLUMS

Even today, I get a small shudder when I think back to the slums at the edge of Mexico City, where, many years ago, my car broke down. As I was driving, the car's engine suddenly died, and I had to let the car roll to the side of the street. My small car was immediately surrounded by a group of young men, tattooed in vivid colors and patterns. They were also casually playing with their switchblade knives.

Tenements lined both sides of the street, as far as the eye could see. Trash cans had been knocked over, and trash littered the sidewalks. On the charred remnants of a lawn was a flaming pile of car tires. It was an area I did not want to be in. But now, life had brought me here, and the eight or ten young men that were surrounding my Honda had already started knocking on the doors and windows with their fists. The "Yankee lady" should come out, they were saying.

I took a deep breath, then opened the door and stepped outside.

Immediately, hard fingers tightly gripped my right wrist. I had to lean my head way back to see the face of the gang leader who had pulled me close to him; he obviously wanted to enjoy my fear and the admiration of the other gang members. But I did not do him the favor of showing fear. In truth, I felt sick with panic. But I didn't show signs of worry for my physical well-being, or for the checks and credit cards in my purse.

Instead, I stared at the gang leader, who was a thin young man with penetrating eyes and an inverted crucifix tattooed on his forehead. I stared straight into his eyes, fully concentrating, but as calmly as possible. During my first quick glance, I had been able to see that while his aura was bright red at the edges, it also showed a lot of gray spots and scars. The boy evidently suffered from an acute lack of energy. And no matter what he was going to ask of me—money, submission, my car—in truth he needed nothing more than life energy.

The Wave of Love

And so I *smiled* at him. I created a feeling of love inside me—selfless, empathetic love for this ragged gang leader who had certainly survived terrible things in his short life. I could feel the love inside me turn into a wave; I could feel my internal gates opening, while all the channels inside me started to fill with love, a tremendous wave of strong life energy, which I then unleashed all at once onto my attacker.

I was still smiling when the gang leader, as if in a trance, released my hand. On his face, there was now a smile that did not necessarily seem intelligent, but it was definitely harmless, even childish. I continued to focus on the feeling of love

> Love is the strongest power in the universe. Love is pure life energy.

toward him, selfless, almost devotional love. Again I felt a wave of energy passing from me to him.

"José," he ordered in a hoarse voice, "you know about cars. Fix this lady's car!"

I forced myself to continue steering energy in his direction. I would have loved to give a small extra portion of my life energy to José as well, but I could feel my reserves depleting rapidly. Luckily, José followed the orders of his startled leader. He had only to plug in a loose cable under the hood, and just a few minutes later, I was back in my car and driving off.

Love Conquers Hate and Violence

The gang leader probably to this day does not understand what happened to him during that confrontation: I had recognized that he suffered from a lack of energy and therefore wanted to rob me of my life energy. Thus, I decided to "voluntarily" let my energy flow in his direction. In other words, I had told myself to love this dangerous young man with all my heart, selflessly. That, and my well-filled energy reserves, allowed me to literally drown him with my love, to flood him with my life energy. This momentarily froze his aggressive tension, and his mind was dazed for a few minutes by the emotions that had overcome him.

But I could not have maintained this self-destructive flow of energy for much longer than a few minutes. If José had needed more than a few minutes to fix my car, I would have fallen on the ground like an empty, flaccid balloon. At the very least, the gang leader, frustrated by the depletion of this energy stream, would have turned back to his usual methods of robbery.

Later on, alone in my car, I cried: I cried from exhaustion and from the suppressed panic that now came out, but I also cried out of gratitude for my rescue and a strange feeling of "holy triumph." Even though I cannot recommend that my clients and readers use this means of defense in similar circumstances, this incident does show that the major religions are right in their message of love: love is the strongest power in the universe, for love is pure life energy.

Those who can find access to this reservoir of energy will immediately be able to stop aggression, which also demonstrates that almost all acts of aggression and conflict between people is about this most valuable commodity of the universe: life energy.

CASE STUDY: AURA PROTECTION AGAINST SEXUAL HARASSMENT

Jessica R. was in her late twenties when she turned to me seeking spiritual energy and life counseling. Jessica worked as a nurse with various evening and night shifts. On a regular basis she had to traverse a poorly lit footpath crossing a park between her apartment and the hospital. This park had high trees, thick hedges, and many winding paths. The park had, on numerous occasions, been the scene of unpleasant events: people had been robbed or threatened with knives, and park visitors, usually women, had been sexually harassed.

During the summer when Jessica came to see me for the first time, she had already experienced some unpleasant situations in the park. A man had jumped out of the bushes in front of her, and had turned and run away only at the last minute. Another time, she saw shadows of people approaching from the upcoming bend in the path, but as she got closer to the people they suddenly ran away in all directions.

The reports of this young woman, who was concerned but not frightened, strengthened the diagnosis I had established after the first analysis of her aura: Jessica R. was a strong, confident person with a healthy, oval-shaped aura in which magenta (will power) and strong shades of blue (thoughtfulness) were dominant.

Still, her concerns about being harassed, or meeting other harm, in the park were valid—especially since these worries were starting to provide an area of attack (her subconscious) for possible energy thieves.

Aside from some conventional precautions (such as pepper spray and avoiding the park when alone at night if possible) and the aura-strengthening exercises provided in chapter three, I also recommended the emergency variant of the pillar-of-light exercise. Those who have learned to visualize this pillar of light spontaneously are usually well equipped to defend themselves against immediate aggression. However, it is critical to be able to surround oneself with the impenetrable pillar of light in one thought—the same fraction of a second during which an aggressor is choosing his victim.

EXERCISE 1: SPONTANEOUS VISUALIZATION OF THE PILLAR OF LIGHT

With your spiritual eye, visualize the pillar of light descending upon you. Observe how quickly this axis of life, made up of pure energy, descends upon you. Feel how the walls of rays descend along your body like shooting arrows.

Make yourself aware that the pillar of light is surrounding you, without any gaps and without room for penetration. Look the aggressor in the eye through the invisible pillar wall—calmly, with the certainty that he or she will not be able to harm you. Repeat to yourself:

"The pillar of light envelops and protects me.
Only positive energies can penetrate
this pillar of light."

Feel yourself floating up to the top of your pillar of light, where your higher self awaits you. Upon arriving to the top of your pillar of light, merge with your higher self and feel its wisdom and power. From this height, observe the potential aggressor: usually he will turn away at this point, since he will (most often subconsciously) recognize that you are not within his reach as a victim.

After the Emergency

Before you float back to the ground inside the pillar, you should thank your higher self for its protection. When you reach the ground, allow the walls of your light pillar to return to the heavens. Breathe, smell, and listen to the sounds of physical reality. Feel how great it is to be alive in this world. And how wonderful it is to be able to get in touch with your higher self at any point in time.

Several months after Jessica R. visited me for the first time, a large man confronted her at night in the park. "He seemed to have appeared out of nowhere," recalled the nurse. "While he was still staring at me, I quickly called upon the pillar of light to descend. Then I walked on, surrounded by the impenetrable walls of rays. I would have walked right through him if he, at the last minute, had not stepped aside, with a look of total incomprehension on his face."

Since then, Jessica R. has never again been harassed. Not in the park, nor anywhere else.

SPONTANEOUS EXTENSION OF YOUR AURA TO PROTECT OTHERS

The means of defense that I introduce in this section assumes that you have enough psychological and physical energy to perform this exercise safely. The further along we are on our spiritual path of growth, the more easily we can extend our aura beyond our self. We can do this without using up our energies. In this way, we can, temporarily, protect those in our care—especially small children, as well as those who are sick or defenseless—against attacks by energy vampires.

Very young children, until about the age of three, are under the aura protection of their mothers (or any other constant caretaker). What is pictured in early paintings one can still visualize today, if one has activated the ability to see auras: the maternal aura surrounds the newborn, who does not yet have an aura of his or her own.

> Toddlers enjoy aura protection from their mothers.

As the child grows over the years, the shared aura of mother and child continues to expand, until in the third or fourth year the child develops his or her own, initially fragile, aura. In the subsequent years, the two auras start to separate, until the child, at the age of five or six, potentially has his or her own aura protection.

However, the aura of children at this age—and until the age of fourteen or fifteen—is still fairly weak and can usually be penetrated easily by adult attackers. Similarly, old or sick people, or veterans who have had traumatic wartime experiences, have auras with weaker defenses, which in some cases can also have holes or scars.

When we are taking care of children, or elderly or sick people, and suddenly see that an attack by an energy vampire could be imminent, it may be necessary to expand the protective shield of our aura to those under our care.

EXERCISE 2: EXTENDING YOUR AURA TO PROTECT OTHERS IN AN EMERGENCY

If you want to extend your protective aura to an infant or toddler, pick the child up and hold her in your arms. Press the child against you. If you want to extend the protection of your aura to a sick or elderly adult, put your arm around that person.

Take a few deep but rapid breaths and feel how your aura is rapidly expanding. Like a wide coat or a large blanket, it envelops you and the people in your care. Make yourself aware of how your aura is completely and entirely surrounding you and those under your care.

Watch how the shining white surface of your aura begins to crystallize: it remains transparent like water that freezes during the winter, but is as impenetrable as bulletproof glass.

Repeat, out loud or to yourself, several times:

"My aura protects me and those in my care.
We are free of all harm."

After the Emergency

Without taking your arms off those in your care, take a few slow and regular breaths. Feel how your aura contracts every time you exhale until it once again tightly surrounds your body. Now, slowly let go of the person you were holding.

PART TWO

Securing the Locks

i n this section, I explain how you can cleanse your chakras and your subconscious by performing simple exercises. You will also learn how to protect yourself against specific kinds of energy attacks.

Many of us, over the past years, have learned exercises to open our chakras; we will now learn exercises to *close* them when we need to do so. Using my directions, you will be able to create a protective space for yourself—which will help defend you against any attacks by energy vampires— and learn to call your spiritual caretaker, who will ensure your safety, day and night.

5 Learning to Close and Protect Your Chakras

Over the past years and decades, an increasing number of people in the West have rediscovered their spirituality. Through meditation, healthy diets, shamanic practices, and many other consciousness-expanding exercises, we have learned to increase our energy levels and to harmonize our material body with the subtle bodies of energy.

The key components in this harmonization process are the chakras, the crossing points between energy bodies and our physical body. People with active psychic abilities—those they kept and developed even after childhood—are easily able to recognize the chakras within the aura. But even those who have only recently rediscovered their ability to see auras are able, using a few exercises, to recognize these subtle centers of energy, which are part of the energy mantel of every living being.

ORDER AND FUNCTION OF THE CHAKRAS

Just as there are different esoteric schools of thought on the dimensions of the aura, there is also debate about the number and hierarchy of the chakras. That, however, is not something that concerns us at this point. In my experience, the most successful exercises have been based upon the seven chakras of classic teachings from the Eastern spiritual traditions. These are divided inside the human aura along a line that runs down from the scalp along the spine in the following manner (see figure 4):

- *Sahasrara,* the crown chakra
- *Ajna,* the pineal, or third-eye chakra
- *Vishuddha,* the throat chakra
- *Anahata,* the heart chakra
- *Manipura,* the solar plexus chakra
- *Svadhishthana,* the navel, or pelvic chakra
- *Muladhara,* the root chakra

If you are not yet able to see the chakras in your aura or in the auras of others, it is sufficient to visualize these centers of energy as small wheels of colored light or circles of flower petals that rotate around a center of gentle white light. The faster a chakra spins, the more energy is being created or transferred into that particular region of the physical body. I have often seen chakras spinning so fast that they appear almost immobile; all one can see is a shining wreath of lights around a "white hole." This white hole then emits sparks of light: it is a lock that has been opened between the physical and the spiritual world, through which precious cosmic energy enters, but which can also be an access point for energy parasites.

On the other hand, chakras that are blocked or can move only slowly

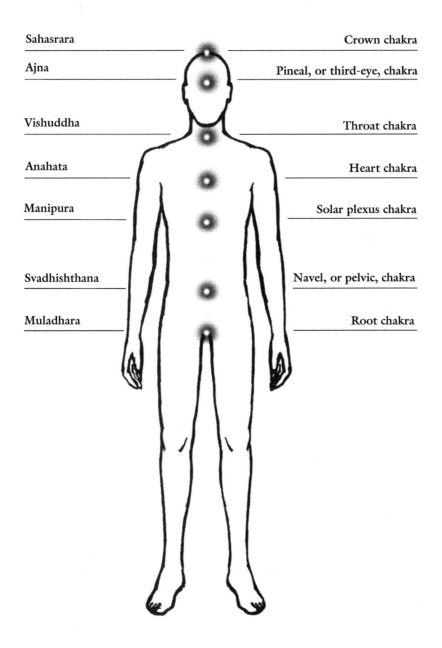

Sahasrara — Crown chakra

Ajna — Pineal, or third-eye, chakra

Vishuddha — Throat chakra

Anahata — Heart chakra

Manipura — Solar plexus chakra

Svadhishthana — Navel, or pelvic, chakra

Muladhara — Root chakra

Figure 4. The seven chakras

resemble black or gray spots in the rays of our aura. These blocked points can also be points where energy thieves can enter our energy field, since at these points the defenses that were gained by aura strengthening will fail.

Just as our physical organs can get sick and not function properly, the functioning of our chakras also depends on their health. Two particular risks are worth mentioning:

➐ When chakras together don't generate enough life energy, the gradual erosion of energy will wear out the affected individual, who often is not aware of the problem. Thus, it is possible that the chakras that are responsible for sexual and emotional energy (heart, solar plexus, navel/pelvic) will not work properly. The result: the individual will constantly be exhausted and feel weak. He will be unable to be enthusiastic about a task, to love himself and others, and so on.

➐ The energy generation and distribution *between* chakras must be optimized for us to realize our potential on all levels. For example, if the navel/pelvic chakra generates significantly more energy than the higher chakras (crown, third eye, throat), we will be forever desiring one thing or another and unable to develop emotions like empathy or sympathy. Thus, we will be unable to develop the spiritual dimensions of our life and our psyches. On the other hand, if someone has a blocked root chakra, the individual will lack grounding and thus be in danger of losing touch with earthly realities.

For understandable reasons, energy vampires prefer victims who have learned to increase their energy levels through regular meditation or other techniques. By opening and stimulating particular chakras, these meditators are able to increase their energy levels without limits. Experienced energy thieves can sense, even at a great distance, the bubbling source of energy, which they recognize as their opened chakras. If we do not take special precautions to repel these energy vampires, those of us who meditate resemble precious gems that lie on the side of the road, sometimes attracting thieves by sparkling and shining in the sunlight.

Just as much at risk are professional counselors, healers, and helpers, whose chakras are wide open as they practice their professions. In this way, they are able to connect intuitively with the thoughts and feelings of their clients. But if they do not intentionally close their chakras afterward, there is a danger that this "lock," and the connection to the client or patient, will remain open. Because these clients or patients have generally turned to helpers or healers as a result of energy blocks, a lack of energy, or related problems, this can lead to serious problems. The life energy can flow from the healer to the client like a transfusion, with the patient making rapid—but false—improvements, while the healer exhausts his or her energy.

Third parties can also take advantage of a healer's failing to close his or her chakra, as shown in the following example from my work.

CASE STUDY: THE VAMPIRE AT MY SIDE

When Tiara Y. asked for my help as a spiritual energy and life consultant, this woman in her late forties had almost exhausted her energies. She had worked as a shaman healer in an institute for holistic life experience and consciousness development for years. Many of her clients were people with life-threatening illnesses (such as cancer) who had been treated in the local hospital; most had been released with pessimistic prognoses, and many were considered terminally ill by traditional medical standards.

Yet Tiara had developed a special energy-building program for these people with serious physical illnesses. Even though her extensive efforts to help sometimes came too late, in some cases she was able to achieve what had been thought impossible. She was able to provoke so-called spontaneous healing, or as the local press called it, "miracles," through the targeting of certain chakras and stimulation of those in areas of the body that had suffered the worst of the illness, as well as visualizing the healing process in shamanic trance rituals, and a host of other techniques.

This brought her fame beyond the narrow confines of her hometown.

Her work, however, was exceedingly exhausting. During the sessions, Tiara consciously steered her life energy to her patients to strengthen them until they were able to produce life energy with their own resources. It was only because Tiara meditated on a regular basis and was able to recharge her own energy resources continually, using spiritual techniques, that she was able to work successfully for years at her institute without suffering physical or psychological harm.

Until the day she met Paul.

After an unhappy marriage, Tiara had lived by herself for ten years and only occasionally allowed herself a small adventure. To her own surprise (and to the shock of those who cared about her), her relationship with Paul seemed from the very beginning to be more than a short-term affair. Paul was fifteen years younger, and although he called himself an artist, he almost never worked. Just a few weeks after Tiara met him, he moved into her spacious apartment and immediately started making himself at home in her rooms and in her life. Usually Tiara was able to see precisely the motivations of others and to recognize their large and small flaws (among her friends she was known for her ability to see people for what they were). These talents, however, seemed to fail her when it came to Paul. To those close to her, it was clear that Paul used Tiara to avoid working and that he tricked her into becoming increasingly dependent on him. Tiara's friends and colleagues observed with great concern how Paul started bossing her around, how he quickly gained power over her. While Paul seemed to flourish, Tiara increasingly suffered from "inexplicable" exhaustion.

For months Tiara angrily dismissed all criticism of her lover and her relationship, although even she had become increasingly concerned, since she, as she later told me, started "changing in the strangest ways" as soon as she was around Paul. At work she was a confident and sympathetic modern woman, yet at home in the shared apartment she changed into a submissive creature without strength or will power. She allowed Paul to order her around and tried to anticipate his every wish.

Paul, however, who passed the many hours Tiara spent at work doing nothing in the darkened apartment, seemed to flourish as soon as Tiara was around him. As soon as she came home, he turned into a charismatic person of great intelligence with a tyrannical will.

Once I had learned these details about Paul and Tiara's relationship, I knew that this was a clear-cut case of a power vampire at work: Paul regularly made Tiara conform to his wishes, thus forcing her to let him take her life energy. He himself suffered from a chronic lack of energy (due to a leak in his aura or a blocked chakra), which explained his vegetating at home while he waited for Tiara's return (like a vampire in a dark basement who waits for the sun to set). Unable to quench his thirst for energy with his own powers, he had to feed on Tiara's, which clearly accounted for the chronic spiritual and physical exhaustion that Tiara had started to suffer since living with Paul. Tiara's high level of energy, which developed through her profession and her spiritual consciousness, had attracted an energy vampire—just like the gem on the roadside attracts thieves by sparkling and shining in the sun.

I tried to share my conclusion with Tiara as gently as possible: "In my view, Paul is a power vampire who is constantly sapping your life energy. Perhaps I'm wrong, but in that case you will do him neither injustice nor harm if you follow the guidelines I'm going to give you now."

I then recommended my program for the conscious closing of the chakras. From then on, Tiara performed a few simple exercises that closed and protected her chakras every night before going home.

Sure enough, things happened as I expected: Tiara was now able to face Paul without feeling weak and submissive. It was as if a veil had been lifted: she was able to see what a weak little tyrant Paul was. Moreover, once he realized that he would no longer be able to get energy from her, he quickly said good-bye and disappeared from her life.

Tiara has since rounded out her program for opening and activating the chakras with some exercises to close them as well. And she has never again been bothered by an energy vampire. She continues to give her energy generously to those in her care, to give them the therapeutic help they need to be able to help themselves. She simply takes the necessary precautions so that no one can tap into her life energy any longer.

Not long after Paul left her life, Tiara met Robert, a talented, good-looking, and successful man her age, with whom she has been living for a few months now. "Robert and I are equal partners," she recently told me, overjoyed. "We complement each other, and our relationship has brought a growth of consciousness, self-confidence, and a joy of living—and a growth of energy."

EXERCISE 1: OPENING THE CHAKRAS

Go to a place where you can lie down comfortably and where you know you won't be disturbed. Lie on your back (on either the floor, a couch, or your bed) and breathe in and out slowly and regularly until you can feel your body relaxing and your attention turning to the world inside you.

Imagine seven magical flowers shining in the most brilliant colors along your spine and in a line past it to the top of your head. In the Far Eastern tradition, these would be lotus flowers, but you may imagine any of your favorite flowers. Take a good look at these flowers and their surroundings with your spiritual eye: some people will picture their flowers growing grouped together in a large meadow, while others may see their chakras as a row of water lilies on the surface of a small creek that flows through a gentle, sloping landscape.

Feel how the sun, that powerful source and transformer of cosmic energy, shines its warming rays along the line on which your flowers grow.

Feel how these rays first touch the lowest flower: the root chakra, Muladhara. Under the sun's rays, its petals open wide.

The rays of the sun then move on, and you can feel them on the navel/pelvic chakra, Svadhishthana. Again, your chakra's petals open wide under the sun's touch.

Slowly and carefully, the sun's rays move on; you can feel them reach the solar plexus chakra, Manipura, and shine on this third flower—once again opening the petals wide.

The sun's rays continue to move slowly along the row of your chakra flowers. Feel the sun reaching the heart chakra, Anahata—gliding over the fourth flower, causing its petals to open wide.

The sun slowly moves on and touches the throat chakra, Vishuddha, again opening its petals with its strong rays.

Slowly, the sun's rays continue along the line of your chakra flowers. Feel the sun gliding over the third-eye chakra, Ajna, and feel its petals opening.

The sun glides on and you can feel its rays above the Sahasrara chakra as its petals open wide under the strong warmth.

Ending the Exercise, Repetition

Remain still for a few moments and feel the petals of your seven chakras circle their wide-open centers. Feel the cosmic wind, the rushing energy of life, which is being directed into your body and soul.

Repeat this exercise as often as you want. It fits best as an addition to regular meditation or other spiritual practices. But do not forget to round it out with the following exercises, especially the exercise for closing (and, if necessary, the exercise for protecting) your chakras.

EXERCISE 2: CLEANSING THE CHAKRAS

After you have opened all your chakras with the first exercise, you should examine your chakras to see whether they are dirty or blocked.

Imagine a hair dryer in your spiritual hand, a small device that instead of blowing air sprays a strong current of white sparks of light. Position this imaginary device close to your root chakra and direct the current toward the inside of the flower. Repeat this cleansing until the petals rapidly and freely rotate toward the center and the center emits sparks as bright as those from the "dryer" in your hand.

Repeat this cleansing for each of the remaining chakras:

Position the dryer close to the petals of your pelvic/navel chakra and direct the current inside the flower. Guide it to the solar plexus chakra, then the heart and throat chakras, each time blowing the sparks of your dryer into the center of the flowers until the petals rotate freely and rapidly and you can see white sparks of lights coming forth from the centers.

End the exercise with the third-eye and crown chakras.

Ending the Exercise, Repetition

Continue to lie still for a few more minutes. Observe all of your chakras and feel the cosmic wind; the turbulent life energy that is being generated by the open and cleansed energy centers is being transferred into your physical body.

Carry out the third exercise as needed. If you do not want to close your chakras at this point, open your eyes and slowly return to the external world.

Repeat this second exercise as a follow-up to the first one whenever you have the feeling that one or several of your chakras might be blocked or dirty.

EXERCISE 3: CLOSING THE CHAKRAS

If you are carrying out this exercise as a direct follow-up to either of the two previous exercises, you may skip to the next paragraph. Otherwise, go to a place where you can lie down comfortably and where you know you won't be disturbed. Lie on your back and breathe in and out slowly and regularly, until you can feel your body relaxing and your attention turning to the world inside you.

Once again, imagine seven magical flowers shining in the most brilliant colors along your spine and in a line past it to the top of your head. In the Far Eastern tradition, these are lotus flowers, but you may choose any of your favorite flowers. Take a good look at these flowers and their surroundings with your spiritual eye: for some of us, these flowers grow in a group in a large meadow, while others see their chakras as a row of lilies on the surface of a creek that flows through banks of light.

Watch as the sun recedes from the flowers. The rays slowly move down along your chakra line in the opposite direction from its pattern in exercise 1. Watch the sun's rays pass over each petal. You can feel its rays touching your crown chakra and the petals of the chakra closing softly yet firmly.

The sun's rays continue to move slowly along the line of your chakra flowers. You feel the sun over the flower of your third-eye chakra and, again, feel its petals closing softly yet firmly.

Carefully, the sun moves on. You feel its rays over the throat chakra and feel your flower's petals closing softly yet firmly.

The sun's rays slowly move on down the row of chakra flowers. Feel how the sun touches the heart chakra and, again, feel the flower's petals closing softly yet firmly.

The sun descends along the line of your flowers and you can feel it reach the solar plexus chakra. Again, you feel the flower's petals closing softly and securely.

The sun moves on at a leisurely pace and you can feel its rays reach the navel/pelvic chakra. Once again, your petals close softly and securely.

The sun slowly continues downward until it reaches the lowest of your row of chakra flowers. You can feel the sun's rays over your root chakra, its petals closing softly and securely.

Ending the Exercise, Repetition

After you have closed your chakras, remain still for a few more moments and absorb the atmosphere of security and comfort. Repeat to yourself several times, either out loud or inside your head:

> *"All of my seven chakra flowers are closed*
> *firmly. My energies will stay with me—*
> *unless I want to share them*
> *with another person."*

Now open your eyes and slowly return to the external world.

You should carry out this exercise daily, or as many times as you feel the need, if the following characteristics describe you:

- You are a healer or helper by profession.
- You meditate or carry out other spiritual exercises on a regular basis.
- You have a suspicion that an energy vampire is trying to use you as a source of energy.

EXERCISE 4: PROTECTING THE CHAKRAS

Perhaps you have the feeling that even after closing your chakras as described in the previous exercise, you are still vulnerable to attacks by energy vampires. Even though I don't think that additional preventive measures are necessary, there is nothing wrong with raising your sense of security through another security-enhancing exercise.

If you add this fourth exercise directly after the third one, please skip to the next paragraph. Otherwise, go to a place where you can lie down comfortably and where you know you won't be disturbed. Lie on your back (on either the floor, a couch, or your bed) and breathe in and out slowly and regularly, until you can feel your body relaxing and your attention turning to the world inside you.

Once again, picture your chakras as a row of flowers in shining colors. After your completion of the preceding exercise, these flowers are closed, and the setting is dusk. The moon has risen, but the sun, a powerful medium of energy and wisdom, still remains on the horizon, its rays shining onto your flowers almost horizontally.

Observe how the low moon is enveloping your chakra flowers in a horizontal pillar of white light. Imagine that you are holding a magic wand in your spiritual hand. Swing the wand over the chakra flowers in flowing movements and repeat several times, either out loud or to yourself:

"Pillar of light, turn into bulletproof glass."

Observe how the horizontal pillar of light turns into glass. As the moon slowly rises toward the sky, it shines onto the row of your closed chakra flowers, which are now additionally encased in a transparent pillar of massive bullet-proof glass.

Ending of the Exercise, Repetition

Remain lying down with your eyes closed for a few more minutes and absorb the atmosphere of complete security. Repeat the following several times, either out loud or to yourself:

> *"All my seven chakra flowers are firmly*
> *closed and protected behind bulletproof glass.*
> *I am absolutely safe."*

Now open your eyes and slowly return to the external world.

6 Cleansing the Subconscious of Psychic Garbage

as previously stated: For all people, things, or situations that we attract in the external world, there are complementary elements inside us. These internal energies shape external circumstances. This means that in our external world we will not attract those people or situations that are unsuited for us if we can let go of the negative energies stored inside us—and if we can prevent creating new negative energies.

The easiest and most efficient way to clean up our internal junkyard is through a ritual cleansing of our subconscious. Most people have deposited unpleasant events in their psychic junkyards: embarrassing memories, unacceptable desires, and so forth. Since only very few people are able to accept themselves completely and thus acknowledge every single deed, thought, or feeling from their past, most people, over the years, accumulate a large amount of psychic garbage.

In cleaning out our subconscious minds, however, the purpose cannot be to "forget" aspects of our selves deemed unacceptable. Rather, we want to take a fresh look at all that has collected in our psyches over the years. In many cases, we will see that we have long since conquered our old weaknesses, which will allow us to part with these memories. In other cases, we will see that we can now integrate in our current selves what we pushed and locked away for so long. The more we are able to accept ourselves as a whole, with all our strengths and weaknesses, light and dark sides, and to accept the angel as well as the dragon in us, the less we will attract energy vampires or offer them areas of attack through which they can get inside us.

CASE STUDY: THE THIEF INSIDE

Peter D. was a successful thirty-five-year-old middle manager in a large car company. He was married with two children, and his life could have been completely in order if it weren't for the bad luck that seemed to follow Peter everywhere he went. If, for example, he went to a convention and parked his car alongside those of a dozen colleagues in an unguarded parking lot, you could be sure that his car would be the only one that would get broken into—even though some of his colleagues had much more expensive cars. If a gang of burglars was operating in Peter's neighborhood, *his* home would be broken into—even though he, unlike his neighbors, had installed an expensive alarm system.

Events such as these happened to Peter at every turn: in restaurants his coat would get stolen or exchanged for a coat of lesser quality. The insurance scammer waiting at an intersection to provoke an accident would hit the gas exactly when Peter was passing by. The dishonest cashier at the supermarket picked Peter out of the line of customers—and charged the expenses of her shopping spree to him. This and more kept happening.

How do you explain such a string of mishaps and bad luck? Those of us familiar with the cosmic laws of energy exchanges, as well as the attraction and transformation of energies, will know the answer. After listening to Peter's story, I asked him flat out: "Is there something in your past, Peter, that has to do with burglary or thieving, I mean, a dark spot where perhaps *you* were the burglar or thief?"

This question was followed by an extended silence. At first, Peter had appeared as though he was about to jump up at the accusation, but he quickly fell back. With an increasingly guilty look, he finally mumbled, "How . . . did you know? It doesn't matter, Dorothy, the fact is, you're right. There was something . . . more than once . . . many years ago. . . . I've never wanted to admit it—not even to myself. . . ."

From looking at Peter's groomed, professional appearance, one would not have suspected what he now admitted: back in his youth and even in his early adulthood, he had often shoplifted in stores and supermarkets. In my view, he still suffered from mild but significant kleptomania. He had never stolen valuable items and had afterward always suffered overwhelming feelings of embarrassment. His acts were entirely unacceptable to him and as inexplicable as the random criminal acts of a stranger. Later on, Peter learned to suppress his self-destructive urge. The worry of returning to his old ways was cause enough for Peter to avoid dealing with these memories, even in fleeting thoughts.

> Suppressed psychological material becomes a magnet for bad luck.

This avoidance, however, caused the memories of his petty thefts—along with his suppressed kleptomania—to land in his psychological junkyard, where they rusted for years. Peter had never before dared to look at these "horrible acts" calmly, let alone tell his wife or a friend. Thus, this suppressed psychological material became a magnet for bad luck, a knot of negative energy anchored in his subconscious. This knot continued to attract those things, people, and circumstances that reflected its negative polarity—that is, thieves, burglars, and bad situations—which, in turn, facilitated the work of those dishonest people.

The advice I gave to Peter was thus simple: "Admit your thievery to yourself," I told him. "Don't hide what you did in the past. Try to look calmly at the person you were back then, and at the things you did. Do you really think you would do them again today?"

Again he was silent for a while.

"No, I don't think so," he finally answered. "I've actually long known that this urge to steal things from others stemmed from my feelings of inferiority back then. Even as a young man, I was always afraid that I would never find a well-paying job, a beautiful wife, that no one would ever love and respect me, and so on. But since I've proved the opposite to myself and the world at large over the last couple of years—how can I be afraid to fall back into these old patterns?"

> Many of our subconscious memories and experiences are also stored inside our body.

To free his subconscious once and for all from these and other aspects, which he used to suppress but had by now actually overcome, I recommended the following exercise to Peter D. and asked him to carry it out every two to three days for two weeks.

Two years after Peter sought my counsel (and followed my advice) as a spiritual adviser, he called me and told me how his life had changed: the previous year he had received a big promotion. In recognition of his services, he became a senior manager; he was overjoyed that his life was now harmonious and going according to his wishes. And Peter never again has been bothered by burglars or thieves.

EXERCISE 1: CLEANSING THE SUBCONSCIOUS WITH THE GOLDEN FLEECE

This exercise is generally more effective for *immediate* protection against the external consequences of negative subconscious energies than are the exercises used for consciousness training described in part 1 of this book. In special circumstances, it may be necessary to defend oneself through the use of this type of short-term measure; in the medium- and long-term, however, we will feel thoroughly secure only after we have cleansed our subconscious of *all* psychic garbage.

When carrying out the following exercise, please bear in mind that many of our subconscious memories and experiences are also stored inside our body (nerves, organs, etc.). Cleansing our subconscious is thus a holistic exercise that includes spiritual and emotional, as well as physical, aspects of our selves.

Go to a place of your choosing, where you can lie down comfortably and not be disturbed. Lie flat on your stomach, extending the arms outward and keeping your legs slightly spread.

Close your eyes and slowly and regularly breathe in and out until you feel the physical tension leaving your body and your attention turning to the world inside you.

With your spiritual eye, imagine your personal happy place. In the center of this place is a golden fleece—a soft golden pile of sheep's or ram's wool. You are spread out on top of this pile of wool, on your stomach, with your head facing left or right, whichever you prefer.

Feel how soft and warm the golden fleece is. Observe its intense golden glow with your spiritual eye.

Now feel how you are increasingly sinking into the golden fleece. Feel how the fleece consists exclusively of rays, light, and warmth. Your body and head sink deeper and deeper into the glowing field of energy, which at the same time is starting to float—a large, soft, warm blanket of sheer energy.

The warm rays slowly start to penetrate you as the blanket floats upward; they are passing through your body and, in doing so, cleansing every cell in your body, every fiber of your being, every chamber of your subconscious.

The rays first penetrate your external layer of skin—your legs, chest and stomach, arms, throat, and the side of your face on which you sank into the fleece. The golden fleece continues to float upward, and a comforting warmth streams through you, a feeling of lightness and love, as the fleece continues its upward journey.

If you start feeling long-suppressed adverse memories coming alive inside you, don't be afraid to spend a few moments with them. Feel the pain or sorrow from the past once again, but with the calmness that enables you to say today: In the end, I overcame it all.

All the old burdens, everything you have suppressed, all you have had to overcome, all the old shadows and weaknesses, are taken away by the golden energy fleece as it continues to float upward.

Cleansed of All Toxins of the Past

Now the golden energy fleece is leaving your body, floating out through your back and the back of your head. It pauses above your body for a moment. See the black areas and dark spots that the golden fleece has filtered out of you. These are all the negative energies from which it has cleansed and freed you.

The golden fleece takes all these dark spots with it as it continues to float upward, toward the sky. In the infinite energy pool of the universe, the golden fleece will be cleansed, and it will be ready for you in all its shining purity and cleansing brightness whenever you need it.

Ending the Exercise, Repetition

Remain lying with your eyes closed for another minute. Repeat several times, either out loud or to yourself:

> *"My subconscious is cleansed of all dark areas and spots. There are only positive energies remaining inside me.*
> *I am pure and I am free."*

Now open your eyes, take a deeper breath than usual, and slowly return to your normal state of consciousness.

Repeat this exercise as many times as you intuitively feel necessary.

THE DREAM AND FANTASY DIARY

If you have the feeling that there is psychic garbage remaining in your subconscious, despite repeated cleansing with the golden energy fleece, it is useful to locate this stubborn energy dirt with the help of a dream and fantasy diary.

➐ Get a small notebook that you can leave by your bed at night and keep with you whenever possible during the day.
➐ Every morning, as soon as you wake up, jot down all the memories you have from your previous night's dreams (your notes might include certain key words, a sketch, or a description of a story line, for example).

❯ If needed, try to train yourself to wake up after a dream, even at night. This helps you document your dream recollections more accurately.

❯ If you daydream, perhaps over lunch or during a break at the office, you should again have your diary handy: note all ideas—including strange images and seemingly unrelated ideas—that come to your mind.

❯ Review your notes of the day once a day if possible. The best time for this is at night. Compare your notes and sketches with those of previous days. All scenes, figures, images, ideas, and so forth that repeatedly appear in your dreams or daydreams or that caused the strongest feelings inside you could lead you to the trail of the psychic garbage you are looking for.

Over time, this method will allow you to locate your psychic garbage as precisely as Peter D. was able to do in the previously mentioned case study. Once you have discovered the damaging part in your subconscious, please continue with the second exercise to cleanse your subconscious.

EXERCISE 2: FOCUSED CLEANSING OF THE SUBCONSCIOUS WITH THE SHOWER OF LIGHT

This exercise is especially useful when you are trying to get rid of "leftover energy pollutants" that perhaps you discovered using a dream and fantasy diary. In contrast to the holistic cleansing with the golden fleece, this is a supplementary exercise for the focused cleansing of specific damage.

Go to a place of your choosing where you won't be disturbed. It would be best if this protected place were your bathroom or near your bathroom.

Sit or lie down in a comfortable position. Close your eyes and breathe in and out slowly and regularly until you can feel your physical tension dissolving and your attention turning to your internal world.

Try to picture the piece of psychic garbage you found (the suppressed memory or weakness) as vividly as possible and try to sense where inside you it might be physically located.

Is the item in question inside your stomach? Is it pressing on your soul (chest, heart)? Does it give you a headache? Look for it until you find the spot—or spots—where it has left its mark.

Cleansing Shower of Energy

Now open your eyes, take off your clothes, and go into the shower. Adjust the water to a comfortable temperature and step under it.

Take the showerhead in your hand and imagine that it is a shower of light that cleanses your energy. Cleansing energy is coming out of the shower in white drops of light.

Direct the shower of light to the part of your body you identified, as well as to the chakra of that body area. Thoroughly cleanse the area by massaging it with the shower of light.

Visualize the golden drops of light penetrating your skin, flushing out and cleaning each cell in your body.

Make yourself aware of how this shower of light is washing out this energy dirt that has nested inside you for so long.

Watch the drops run down along your skin and disappear down the drain. From there they will reach the infinite energy pool of the universe, where they will be cleansed and available to you whenever you need cleansing again.

Ending the Exercise, Repetition

Turn off the shower and towel yourself dry. Using the towel, massage the body area that you just cleansed with the shower of light.

Repeat several times, either out loud or to yourself:

"My subconscious now has also been cleansed
of [name your pollutant]. There are
only positive energies inside me.
I am pure and I am free."

If necessary, repeat this exercise once a day until you feel sure that you are completely free of every energy pollutant.

7 Create Your Own Spiritual Safe Area

those who meditate or use other techniques to develop their consciousness or energy levels always run the danger of being attacked by energy thieves during these periods of spiritual openness.

Moreover, people in certain professions—healers, helpers, and people in creative endeavors—are at increased risk of becoming the victims of attacks by energy vampires, since they need to open their energy centers to carry out their work. To engage in our usual spiritual practices and professions without danger, it is therefore recommended to take certain precautions. Such precautions should do more than shield our aura and protect our

> Those who meditate need a safe area.

chakras, they should also protect the physical space in which we meditate or work with an impenetrable shield of light.

These protective measures are useful not just for those people who are spiritually active, but also for people that, for some reason, fear that they might be attacked by energy vampires—either at work or at home. Those who want to be sure that no unwanted guest strengthens him- or herself with their energy resources should carry out the exercises for the creation of a spiritual safe area that follow the case study.

CASE STUDY: THE INVISIBLE STRAW

When Fiona P., a thirty-three-year-old graphic artist, received a long-term contract from a large advertising agency, she quit her job in the public relations department of a large supermarket chain to start working as a freelancer. Expecting a productive and lucrative new future, she moved into a new apartment, where she would be able to both live and work. She used the same bright and nicely furnished room in which she put her desk and computer to take regular meditation breaks to relax and regain her creativity.

For "inexplicable reasons," as she explained during our first meeting, the move proved to be a "disastrous mistake." Fiona had looked forward to her new apartment, her challenging contract, and her life as a freelance creative artist. Yet from the moment she unpacked and put up her computer across from her meditation corner, she had felt exhausted and depressed. "It's cursed," she said. "As soon as I sit at my desk, I feel tired, empty in my head. And when I try to use meditation to regain strength and develop some new ideas, I have the feeling of spiritual leaking, like a container with holes . . . or perhaps," she added thoughtfully, "like a glass, out of which someone is drinking through an invisible straw."

Images such as those described by Fiona are often very helpful in diagnosing energy problems. Our subconscious does not articulate itself in abstract terms, but rather in concrete images. As such, it offers us important associative hints. It is important to pay attention to these images when, for example, trying to discover why someone suddenly feels unwell or weak.

I asked Fiona whether there was someone in her life about whom she would readily say, "This person drains my strength."

She immediately said no, then fell into a long silence.

I elaborated: "This doesn't necessarily have to do with physical distance or proximity: people can draw on our energy even if we rarely see them in the external world. After all, spiritual contact does not require physical, or even visual, contact."

> Energy vampires don't need to be physically close to you in order to steal your energy.

After I said this, Fiona looked at me with an expression of profound surprise, and I could see shock in her eyes. "There is someone," she stammered, "but I thought . . . that . . . that was long over."

I will summarize what Fiona told me that day in stammers and sighs:

At the supermarket chain where she used to work, Fiona was good friends—though strictly on a platonic basis, she emphasized—with a coworker named Sean. The two had planned to start their own business together, and Sean had initially worked with her on the concept with which they wanted to bid for the project offered by Fiona's current client. They had often met on weekends and at night to work on their sketches and copy, but Fiona became increasingly annoyed with Sean. "He didn't have any ideas or creative energy," she said. "He only criticized my ideas, only to later pass them off as his own."

One night, when Sean, after having drunk several glasses of alcohol, tried to get physical, she kicked him out of her apartment. She spent the following night angry and restless. The next morning she told Sean that she was no longer interested in going into business with him. He reacted with anger. It was true that he, just like Fiona, had already quit his job at the supermarket chain and now had to look for a new job. Still, his anger seemed exaggerated, even frightening to her: it was as if she, Fiona, were not an independent person allowed to change her mind, but rather his property who ought to follow his orders.

"When we last saw each other, about six months ago, he cursed at me. He is a parasite," she told me. "I realized that just in time—otherwise, I would be working with him today, paying his way, while Sean . . ." Again she fell into silence and looked at me, somewhat nervously, yet expectantly.

"If I'm not mistaken," I explained, "then you are doing just that today, Fiona, you are feeding Sean—your parasite, as you rightly describe him. He is a kind of energy tick sucking on your spiritual artery."

In addition to my exercises for aura strengthening (see chapter 3) and for the closing of the chakras (see chapter 5), I recommended keeping a dream and fantasy diary for the next couple of days. This proven aid, which I described in chapter 6, quickly showed that it was indeed Sean who was draining her of life energy through his vampiric attacks. He kept appearing in her dreams and daydreams, and Fiona saw him "secretly drinking from my glass with an invisible straw."

It was clear why there was still such a close energy connection between Fiona and Sean: Fiona had so forcefully suppressed her anger toward her former friend and business partner, as well as her worry about not being able to succeed on her own, that a strong current of negative energy subconsciously continued to connect her with Sean. As for Sean, he had undoubtedly (perhaps unconsciously) planned on thriving at the expense of Fiona's energy and creativity. After their separation, he simply continued tapping her life energy, which he had all along counted toward his own "energy account."

After this case of energy vampirism had been solved, I recommended that Fiona cleanse her subconscious with the golden fleece, as well as with my exercises for the creation of a spiritual safe area, most of which are discussed later on in this chapter. Through this program, Fiona experienced the following results:

➔ Soon after Fiona started visualizing the white fortress (see the following exercise) at night, Sean disappeared from her dreams and daydreams.

➔ After she had also carried out the banning ritual for the creation and cleansing of her spiritual safe area, Fiona received a rush of revitalization and creativity almost overnight.

➔ To be completely secure and to ensure that Sean could never bother her again as an energy parasite, Fiona finally called upon her spiritual guardian under my guidance (see chapter 8). She charged her guardian with the task of immediately alerting her and taking all necessary defensive precautions if Sean or any other energy vampire tried to enter her spiritual safe area.

EXERCISE: THE WHITE FORTRESS

This exercise deals with visualizing spiritual protection in any of our surroundings, as opposed to protecting just a particular physical space. This means that this exercise can also be used in emergencies or for preventive purposes. If, for example, you are staying in an out-of-town hotel or house and you suspect energy vampires in the area, you can use this exercise to protect this area against such parasites.

Choose a comfortable place to sit or lie down, and make sure that you won't be disturbed. Dim the lights and turn off any sources of noise. Close your eyes and slowly breathe in and out until you feel your body relaxing and your attention turning toward your internal world.

With your spiritual eye, imagine the sight of a wide blue sky in which there are a few large white clouds floating along. Take a closer look at one of these clouds: it has the outline of a large, reassuring fortress with high walls and round, solid turrets on the corners.

Observe your "dream castle" as it floats toward you and slowly descends. The closer the fortress gets to you, the brighter its white color shines. As it approaches, become aware that the fortress is only seemingly built out of clouds—in fact, its walls are made out of pure, shining, and bright energy. The walls, turrets, and floors of the fortress are transparent. A massive, transparent roof of energy covers the walls and the interior. As the fortress is descending upon you, you can see through its floor, as well as through its walls and ceiling, with the sky in the background.

Now experience how the white fortress is floating through the roof of the house you are in—and even through the floors above you—until it floats through the ceiling of the room.

Maneuver the fortress with your spiritual eye—and, if necessary, with your spiritual hands—until the walls of the fortress surround the walls of your room, the floor of the fortress is below the floor of your room, and its ceiling is above that of the room. Look around and make sure for yourself that the room you are in is now surrounded entirely by your energy fortress.

Repeat several times, either out loud or to yourself:

*"This room and I are surrounded
by my spiritual fortress. Only positive
energies can reach me."*

Ending the Exercise, Repetition

Remain sitting or lying with your eyes closed for a few more minutes and try to experience the calming security afforded by your fortress of white light as intensively as possible.

Now get up and walk around the room, while making sure to hold on to the feeling of being inside a fortress. Make yourself aware of the fact that your fortress of pure energy continues to surround you—whether you are standing up, sitting, or lying down, whether you are awake or asleep, or your eyes are open or shut.

Repeat this exercise when and wherever necessary. At home or at work, it can be used as an introduction to or amplification of the ritual for the creation of a spiritual safe area; when you are traveling or sleeping away from home, you can surround yourself with the white fortress before going to sleep.

An Emergency Variant

In emergencies, when you have the feeling that an attack by energy vampires is imminent, I recommend that you visualize the fortress descending upon you in a flash and feel the room light up as the walls of rays surround it.

BANNING RITUAL FOR THE CREATION AND CLEANSING OF A SPIRITUAL SAFE AREA

If you have a place (or want to create one) where you meditate on a regular basis, carry out other spiritual practices, or conduct spiritual work, I recommend turning this area into a spiritual safe area, off-limits to energy vampires. You can then perform exercises for the creation of physical and mental energies without worrying about the dangers that arise when you open your energy centers—whether during meditation, while healing or helping others, or during other spiritual activities.

The ritual cleansing of any area will automatically turn it into a spiritual safe area. After we have removed all energy pollutants, the room will no longer contain anything that could attract energy vampires. In principle, we do not treat our spiritual safe area any differently than we do our aura, our chakras, or our subconscious. By removing the "psychic garbage" stored there, we make sure that positive energies can circulate freely. This creates an atmosphere that energy vampires shy away from, just as the legendary blood vampires are said to fear the sun, which, incidentally, could represent the white light of pure positive energy so detrimental to energy parasites.

To completely cleanse our safe area from all energy pollutants, we use the magical elements of esoteric traditions: Spirit, Air, Fire, Water, and Earth.

Set up a table in the center of the room that you want to turn into your spiritual safe area and spread a white cloth on it. Decide on which side of the table you are going to stand for this ritual. You should position yourself such that there is neither a door nor a window behind your back (if necessary, cover doors or windows with a white cloth).

Place the following items on the table (see figure 5 on page 98):

- In the center: a glass ball to symbolize the element Spirit. (Note: Crystal balls can be found in numerous crystal or spiritual shops. You may also use a large gaming marble made of glass as a substitute for a glass ball.) Imagine the table as a clock, with the glass ball as the center, where the clock hands are attached.
- At the three o'clock position there is a bowl with bread crumbs or salt to represent the element Earth.
- In the six o'clock position there is a bowl of water to represent the magical element Water.
- In the nine o'clock position there is a white wax candle next to a pack of matches for the element Fire.
- In the twelve o'clock position there is a bowl with incense that represents the element Air.

It is recommended that you complete the exercise for the cleansing of your aura (see chapter 3) immediately before carrying out this banning ritual. Then move into the room you want to turn into a spiritual safe area and in which you have prepared the symbols for the five magical elements.

Make sure that you won't be disturbed during the ritual. Walk up and down the room for a few moments and concentrate on what you are about to do. Then step onto the spot you chose for yourself at the table, again making sure that neither a door nor a window is behind your back.

Calling the Element Earth

Place your right hand on the bowl with the salt or the bread. Close your eyes and breathe in and out deeply and evenly five times.

Repeat, either out loud or to yourself:

> *"Element Earth, I seek your protection*
> *for this room."*

Open your eyes and take the bowl representing the element Earth into your right hand. In a clockwise circle, walk the outer perimeter of the room in slow, solemn steps.

While you are walking, use your left hand to dispense a small amount of the bread crumbs or salt along the room's perimeter, five times in regular intervals. Each time you dispense some of the element Earth (as represented by the salt or bread) say the following:

> *"The element Earth protects and*
> *cleanses my room."*

Return to the table at the center of the room. Return the empty bowl to its spot and let your left hand rest on it. Repeat, either out loud or to yourself:

> *"Element Earth, I thank you for protecting and*
> *cleansing my room."*

Figure 5. Arrangement of elements for the banning ritual

Take your left hand off the bowl and place it on the table in front of you.

Calling the Element Water

Now place your right hand on the bowl of water, close your eyes, and again take five deep and even breaths. Repeat, either out loud or to yourself:

> *"Element Water, I seek your protection*
> *for this room."*

Open your eyes and take the bowl in your right hand. Holding this bowl representing the magical element Water, walk clockwise along the perimeter of the room in slow, ceremonial steps.

While you are walking, use your left hand to dispense the water five times in regular intervals along the perimeter of your safe area. Each time you dispense the drops of water say the following:

*"The element Water protects and
cleanses my room."*

Now return to the table at the center of the room. Return the empty bowl to its place on the table, and let your left hand rest on the bowl. Repeat, either out loud or to yourself:

*"Element Water, I thank you for protecting and
cleansing my room."*

Remove your left hand from the bowl and place it on the table.

Calling the Element Fire

Light the candle, place your right hand around its shaft, and close your eyes. Again, take five deep and even breaths.

Repeat, out loud or to yourself:

*"Element Fire, I seek your protection
for this room."*

Open your eyes and take the candle with the element Fire in your left hand. Holding the candle, walk clockwise along the perimeter of the room in slow, solemn steps.

While you are walking, gently swing the candle five times in regular intervals and imagine flames extending from the candle into the perimeter of your safe area. Each time you swing the candle say the following:

> *"The element Fire protects and*
> *cleanses my room."*

Now return to the table in the center of the room. Keep the candle burning and return it to its place. While keeping your left hand on the candle, repeat, either out loud or to yourself:

> *"Element fire, I thank you for protecting and*
> *cleansing my room."*

Remove your hand from the candle and place it on the table.

Calling the Element Air

Now light the incense, put your right hand on the bowl, close your eyes, and take five deep and even breaths. Repeat, either to yourself or out loud:

> *"Element Air, I seek your protection*
> *for this room."*

Open your eyes and take the bowl with the element Air in your right hand. Holding the bowl, walk clockwise along the perimeter of the room in slow, solemn steps.

While you are walking, wave the bowl five times in regular intervals with your right hand, so that some smoke of the element Air demarcates the perimeter of your safe area. Every time you wave the bowl say the following:

> *"The element Air cleanses and*
> *protects my room."*

Now return to the table in the center of the room. Return the bowl to its place, and let your left hand rest on top of it. Repeat, either to yourself or out loud:

> *"Element Air, I thank you for protecting and*
> *cleansing my room."*

Take your left hand off the bowl and place it in front of you on the table.

Calling the Element Spirit

Now look at the glass ball in the middle of the table. Without touching the ball, fix your eyes on it and take in its appearance. Close your eyes and take five deep and even breaths. Repeat, either to yourself or out loud:

> *"Element Spirit, I seek your protection*
> *for this room."*

See with your spiritual eye how the ball starts to shine with bright light. Become aware of the ball expanding, steadily getting bigger until it fills your entire room with its light, its rays, and its energy. Feel the warmth, purity, and cleansing of the magical element Spirit, which is taking away every last trace of energy pollution from your room.

Now open your eyes again, look at the ball, and say, either to yourself or out loud:

> *"Element Spirit, I thank you for protecting and*
> *cleansing my room."*

Ending the Exercise, Repetition

To end the ritual lift your arms and extend them over the table, spreading them to form a V. Keep your hands open, with palms facing down, while doing this.

First, fix your eyes on the glass ball, then on the symbols for the elements Earth, Water, Fire, and Air, one after another.

Repeat the following with conviction, either out loud or to yourself:

> *"My spiritual space has now been cleansed and is*
> *safe. Only positive energies can penetrate it."*

It is usually not necessary to repeat the banning ritual. If you are not absolutely sure that your spiritual safe area is completely secure after this ritual, you should repeat the exercises for cleansing and strengthening the aura, as well as those for the cleansing of the chakras and the subconscious. After that, you can repeat the banning ritual if you desire.

8
Ally Yourself with Your Spiritual Guardian

or all people who perform spiritual exercises on a regular basis, it is advisable to keep a dream and fantasy diary (as discussed in chapter 6). This will not only help you in tracking down any energy parasites trying to drain you of your life energy, it will also facilitate the search for your guardian angel, spiritual guardian, or whatever you want to call this being.

USING YOUR DREAM DIARY TO SEARCH FOR YOUR GUARDIAN

If you do not yet know your spiritual guardian, you should try to find out what protective, trustworthy, and powerful figure appears frequently in your dreams and daydreams. Sketch or draw this figure in your diary; write down a description of its appearance and character; and note what your (potential) guardian angel tells you in your dreams, or what you are telling your guardian.

Ask for Your Guardian's Name

When daydreaming, as well as during nighttime dreams, if you are able to control either to this degree, ask for your guardian's name. Ask your guardian to tell you where he or she comes from and why he or she is with you.

Learn the Origins and Mission of Your Guardian

If it turns out that your spiritual guardian has been honored as a god, holy person, or something similar at any point in time and by any culture, you should become familiar with the legend and earthly deeds of this character. Obtain a picture or a sculpture of that character that you can put up in your spiritual safe area as well as take with you if you feel the need for protection.

When you are convinced intuitively that this character is indeed your personal guardian from the spiritual world, you should form a conscious bond with your spiritual guardian or guardian angel using the following short ritual.

EXERCISE: CALLING YOUR GUARDIAN

Retreat to your spiritual safe area and make sure that you won't be disturbed. Sit down in a comfortable position and take deep, regular breaths for a few minutes.

Now meditate on an image of a guardian angel or keeper, be it one that you drew yourself, or one you obtained elsewhere. Become familiar with the image, think about the characteristics you have found out about your guardian: kindness, power, boundless energy as a guardian, and so forth.

Close your eyes and feel the presence of your guardian inside you. Make yourself aware of the energy that your guardian radiates and of the energy that you, in turn, are releasing toward him or her.

Say the following, either out loud or to yourself:

"Welcome, [name of guardian].
Please continue to provide me with
protection and to let me share in your
strength and wisdom.
I turn my spiritual safe area over to you for
safekeeping. Make sure that only positive
energies can enter it.
Thank you."

Remain in a silent dialogue with your personal guardian for a few more minutes. Listen carefully for any answer you might get.

Now open your eyes again and slowly return to your normal state of consciousness.

From now on you will be able to connect with your spiritual guardian whenever you wish. Usually it is enough to silently call your guardian. You can also arrange a sign with him or her, eliminating the need for words. Or, perhaps you want to ask your guardian to get in contact with you as soon as you visualize a given symbol.

PART THREE

Protection against Energy Vampires in Business and the Workplace

i n this part of the book, I use practical examples, exercises, and rituals to show how we
can protect ourselves against energy vampires at our workplace and in the business world. I also wish to address the
positive aspects of working as a group: groups of people
within companies as well as companies as a whole can form
powerful group or corporate auras, which, in principle, can
be strengthened, cared for, and protected just like the aura
of an individual. That is why I will also present exercises for
the protection and strengthening of supra-individual auras.

The much-discussed flows of capital in the world of
business are nothing more than immense streams of energy—
which are therefore intensely fought for. That is why the work
and business world is an especially attractive stage for energy
vampires: nowhere else do they find such gigantic sources of
energy—people, ideas, passions, hopes, wealth—in such
abundance as in corporations and businesses.

Most of us do not spend the majority of our time
with our families or friends, but at work. For the overwhelming majority of people today, this means that one
spends eight hours or more every day in an office where
one is generally surrounded by the same people, whether
colleagues, staff, or bosses. Moreover, often departments
and staff will spend a certain part of their free time together
as well, by going out to eat together, going to see a movie,
or going to sports clubs. But those who, for some reason,
are considered outsiders—be it because they leave the
group, or because the group pushes them away—can often
feel the negative side of the pressure that such a group of

people is able to exert. This pressure can quickly escalate into bullying or mob attacks.

The core of the conflict in these cases is usually a fight for life energy: the mob that falls on a victim, picks on the person, and takes the victim's dignity really acts like a multi-headed energy vampire feasting on stolen life energy. Little wonder then that the victims of mob attacks above all else complain about their feelings of paralyzing weakness and gaping emptiness following such an attack.

A group that works together in offices and departments has—at least partially—the same goals and thus develops a group aura over time, or even a supra-individual team, or group, spirit. Similarly, entire corporations can develop an aura of their own. In some ways, this is what is behind the term *corporate identity*. When the leaders of a corporation are able to direct all energy flow—human resources (i.e., the knowledge and passion of their employees) as well as capital resources—in the same direction, the corporation will indeed gain a life of its own; a powerful "corporate" character will be created that has an aura of its own. If the energy structure—the aura of a department, a team, or the entire corporation—suddenly falls into disarray for some reason, the corporate character can fall apart and sink as quickly as it was once created.

But how do teams "function"? What energy laws are behind the building and dissolution of supra-individual auras? Let us briefly look at the basic energy laws, using the example of successful research or creative teams. I am well aware that in many offices there is less creativity and desire to learn than there is routine and stagnation. Nonetheless, the same energy laws apply in all settings. It is, however, easiest to recognize those laws in places where energy flows are strongest and are being directed in a more conscious manner.

Three Basic Energy Rules for Strong Teams

We live in an age of teamwork. In general, the success of modern businesses is not based on the work of one individual—a.k.a. the lone genius—but rather is based on the grouping of talents among individuals. This is especially true in areas where creative thinking is required. This preference for working with groups has nothing to do with the supposed decline of the individual. On the contrary.

Teams are not a collective in which every member is the same. Rather, the secret to the success of constructive groups is in connecting the specific strengths of individuals into a team character and spirit. This enhances the creative and intellectual potential of each team member and creates a whole that is much greater than the sum of its parts.

However, the specific strengths of a group rely completely on the strongest positive energies that each team member contributes to the group. This forms the first rule defining team energy.

> **FIRST TEAM RULE**
> Team spirit develops from the strongest positive energies that each individual contributes to the group.

Members of a group are willing and able to share their best energies only when everyone respects and values one another. The second rule for team energy is that the members must be aware of their own strengths and know and value those of others. Rivalry within a group is about as effective as a competition between our ears and our eyes over who has better senses. False modesty has no place in a group either: in a team, the members have to work where they are most effective.

> **SECOND TEAM RULE**
> Team spirit requires being conscious of our own strengths and of those of the other team members.

> **THIRD TEAM RULE**
> In the team, all energies are focused on whoever is working.

Everyone can understand the heartening feeling that a person receives if he or she is the focus of attention of a receptive, even enthusiastic, audience. This forms the basis for our third rule. Actors get their energy from the applause of the audience, and in some regards, we are the same: attentive listeners stimulate our mind, wit, and speech, meaning that even the least articulate person can be passionately eloquent under the right circumstances. Individuals are thus capable of much bigger things when their group supports their strongest side through focused attention and energy.

For example, imagine an informal conference of leading corporate managers seeking to identify new markets for their products through a casual brainstorming session. If everyone tries to talk over the rest or to put down the ideas of others, this meeting can lead to nothing but frustration.

And if there is a strict hierarchy, where the most attention goes to the most powerful person, rather than the most creative one, there is little chance for particularly innovative ideas. If, however, the team agrees to support—with all its energy—the member who at the moment has the strongest and most constructive ideas, this team spirit will bring about results of which neither a separately acting CEO nor a bunch of rivaling managers would be capable.

> In hierarchical companies, the person with the most power automatically gets the most energy. In strong teams, all energies flow to the active individual.

Even though this rule may be easy to comprehend in theory, its application in practical situations is hard for decision makers used to hierarchies and competition. In old-fashioned companies, the person with the most power automatically gets the most energy: he has an institutionalized right to pump himself up with the energies of his staff.

In modern companies, which are structured to take into account the laws of energy, all possible energy flows are directed toward the team member (or department, division, etc.) who has the most potential for a given situation. When a different "player" in the group picks up the ball and continues with it using his or her own specific strengths, energies are transferred from the previous player, and all team members—including the previous player—focus their energies on the new key player.

10

When Team Spirit Suffers from a Lack of Energy

U nfortunately, in many offices the team spirit is not altruistic and creative. Existing structures are often too rigid and hierarchical to create an ideal setting for a strong team. This is bad for the company, since a weak—or even energetically negative—team spirit lowers the capacities of the company.

A lack of energy in a group facilitates mob attacks. Moreover, the members of the group themselves will suffer, since a poor group aura is usually a sign of energy fights between competing individuals. Outsiders on the fringes of such groups typically suffer the most from a weak or negatively charged aura, especially if the group turns into a "multiheaded energy vampire" and begins hunting for a victim. After all, groups with a weak or negatively charged aura have one thing in common: a lack of life energy, which affects individual members as much as the team spirit as a whole.

CASE STUDY: FENDING OFF A MOB ATTACK AT WORK

Liza D. was in her late thirties when her husband of ten years left her overnight. In their partnership, she had been the stereotypical model of a woman who sacrifices everything for her man. She did this to such a degree that her husband, Frank (who, according to her descriptions, was a classic narcissist who constantly needed attention), had sucked up all her energies. He had therefore moved on to find a new victim.

When Liza consulted me for the first time, she had the physical appearance of a ghost, or someone who had just barely survived a life-threatening illness. But with the help of the strategies presented in this chapter, as well as the use of the exercises and rituals presented in previous chapters, Liza quickly regained her strength. Even her self-confidence, which had been constantly under attack during her marriage, recovered after several weeks so that Liza was once again ready to resume the "fight with the real world," as she called it. Stated less dramatically, she needed a job.

Even though Liza had a law degree, she had not worked in ten years, and thus had to make several attempts before finding a position in a large real estate office. The department for property sales contracts consisted of twelve people—seven men and five women, including herself. When Liza began her job, in the spring of 1996, there was a strange tension in the department. It did not take long for Liza to realize what was going on: one of her colleagues, a young woman named Marylou who had joined the company a few weeks earlier, was subtly but systematically being bullied and intimidated by the longtime employees.

"There was a real psychological war going on there," Liza told me. "When I asked some of my colleagues what they had against Marylou, they simply shrugged and said, smiling, 'She just has to go.'"

The mob terror against Marylou continued for a few more days until the victim gave up and quit her job. Only then did it hit Liza that the group was now probably looking for its next victim. And she was the only candidate around.

After years with her husband, Liza had significant experience in psychological warfare, and was able to quickly assess the trouble stirring in her direction. Moreover, I had explained the basic spiritual energy concepts to Liza in long conversations, which allowed her to see the reasons behind this aggressive group behavior.

The underlying theme of Liza's department seemed to be—even though people might not have been actively aware of it—*fight for energy*. The head of the department was a chronically ill man in his late fifties; everyone assumed he would resign in the not-too-distant future for health reasons. Three employees who thought they had a shot at the position were constantly watching one another and were trying to get as many colleagues as possible on their respective sides, since traditionally the department head was chosen among the staff. This incessant rivalry of course led the group to disregard all three energy rules, which I outlined in the previous chapter.

- Not one of the three candidates thought about investing his or her specific strengths for the good of the team. On the contrary, they were constantly putting down their rivals as well as their followers.
- Not one of these candidates, or followers, was willing to recognize the strengths of others, and no one was realistically able to evaluate his or her own strengths. Instead, every perception and action was being influenced by the power struggle over the succession of the department head.
- Power struggles and different factions also constricted the flow of energies: no one ever received the attention of the full group; at most, one received only the attention of those in one's faction. Moreover, energy flows did not go toward those who had

the strongest abilities for a certain assignment, but were always directed through hierarchies, or other power structures.

This department would long ago have dissolved into three infighting subdivisions if it had not been for the need to appear as a unit, which ensured the maintenance of a rudimentary team spirit. This team spirit, however, was almost exclusively negative: the group could agree only on rejecting the requests of other departments or higher-ups and on strengthening the power of their department within the company. Thus, it was not just the individual members of the group but the group as a whole that suffered from an acute lack of energy.

Who would be surprised that a negative group spirit would manifest itself in psychological terror against a victim? For a team as disorganized as that of Liza's department, a mob attack was almost the only way to get that invigorating shot of energy. However, the effect was only temporary and only achieved by overwhelming a victim—chasing him or her out of the group like a swarm of mosquitoes surrounding a defenseless hiker.

But Liza's story has a happy ending. After the recent victim, Marylou, left the battlefield and cursed her coworkers, Liza heeded my advice to take the offensive. Instead of waiting to be chosen as the next victim of a mob attack or taking the side of the vampires (in hopes that they would then put their teeth in someone else's throat), she dared a courageous attempt to dampen the aggressiveness of the group spirit.

For her offensive, Liza chose the only method that truly impresses vampires: she showed her teeth. To put it differently, Liza smiled until her jaw ached. She gave as much attention—and thus energy—as she could possibly spare, to every colleague in her department. In doing this, she was careful to ensure that the three faction leaders did not get more energy than their followers, nor did she treat one of the factions better than the rest. She just acted as if she weren't in a splintered group, but rather in a well-organized team that was following the basic energy rules.

Although at first she was the only one to follow these rules, she maintained this exhausting offensive for an entire week, thanks to her well-filled energy reservoirs and her robust aura, both of which she gained and maintained thanks to my production and protection exercises. By constantly giving away energy, she was able to disarm the members of the group. Attempts to initiate the mob behavior toward Liza were deflected by her aura and quickly stopped. Instead, many members of the group came to desire Liza's smiles, interest, and attention: no one else in the department gave away energy as willingly as she.

During the second week, some colleagues began to return her smiles. At the beginning of the second month, Liza and I talked at length about the fact that the divisions between the factions had started to crumble. The three leaders were becoming increasingly isolated. At the end of her seventh week in the department, Liza suggested to all of her colleagues that they start off the weekend by going out to dinner together. She had long prepared for this moment, and while she was waiting for the response, she tried not to let her tension show. Nine colleagues, including Liza, took part in this first dinner. Only the three rivals for the department head position declined to take part in this "fraternization" with the other group members. After all, their power was based on subjugation and fragmentation.

The dinner was a triumph for Liza, and it was the day that a new team spirit was created in the department.

Half a year later the ailing department head finally retired. By this point, two of the three former candidates for the position had quit their jobs, while the third had been transferred to another department. Liza D. was elected department head by an overwhelming majority. Her promotion was lauded by the highest echelons of management—they credited her with the creation of a constructive group dynamic, which had led to a noticeable increase in the overall energy level, motivation, and creativity of the team members.

EMERGENCY CHECK: HOW TO EFFECTIVELY PROTECT YOURSELF AGAINST MOB ATTACKS

Not all of my readers will be able or willing to use an "offensive of smiles." In fact, an offensive defense such as the one employed by Liza D. requires much self-confidence, a robust aura, and an ample supply of energy resources. Moreover, there are a host of reasons why it may be preferable—depending on the situation and one's own professional standing—to employ less visible tactics.

I've compiled some suggestions in this chapter for how you can defend yourself against mob attacks or other types of energy vampirism at your place of work. First, ask yourself the following questions to determine how vulnerable your workplace is to energy vampires.

A QUICK QUIZ TO RATE YOUR WORKPLACE FOR ENERGY VAMPIRES

DOES YOUR WORKPLACE HAVE A CLEAR HIERARCHICAL STRUCTURE WITH A "STRONG" MAN OR WOMAN AT THE TOP?

Such a hierarchy can be an indication of a latent group energy problem—and thus a warning sign for possible mob attacks. As a power vampire, the boss continually takes some of the energies of his or her subordinates, leading the members of the group, in turn, to develop vampiric characteristics in order to maintain their energies by feeding on suitable victims.

DO YOUR COLLEAGUES OR DOES THE PARTICULAR GROUP YOU WORK WITH EXERT A STRONG PRESSURE ON NEWCOMERS TO CONFORM?

Such pressure tends to manifest itself in rigid views and behavior patterns, which are fiercely defended. Thus there might be a forced consensus in the group on which restaurant to eat at during the lunch break (and which restaurant one would never visit), what sports to engage in after work (and what sports are only for idiots), or what kinds of clothes are in style (and what styles mark one as an underdog, show-off, etc.). People new to the office are then faced with the choice of either sharing these views and behaviors or being isolated as outsiders.

DOES THE GROUP YOU WORK WITH DO A LOT OF THINGS TOGETHER, EVEN OUTSIDE OF WORK? IS THE GROUP PRESSURING YOU TO CONFORM WITH ITS ACTIVITIES IN YOUR FREE TIME?

Groups that are characterized by negative traits—such as a shared lack of energy—have a tendency to manipulate the lives of their members, even beyond the professional realm. It is a big warning sign if the group demands rigid display of common interests and excessive participation in outside-of-work activities—playing sports together, going to the movies, taking weekend trips as a group, etc.—or insinuates that everyone must accept the group's convictions and habits, and even adopt them.

ANALYZING THE CHECKLIST

One "Yes" Response

If you answered one of the three questions with "yes," you should be careful. If you let yourself be overwhelmed by the group, you too will start suffering from the lack of energy that is so characteristic of this group. But if you set yourself apart too much, you risk becoming an outsider and thus potentially a victim of the group's existing (or latent) vampiric instincts.

Two "Yes" Responses

If you answered "yes" to two of the three questions, you should take protective measures immediately: it is very likely that this group possesses vampiric traits and a clear energy deficit. You run the danger of being forced to integrate yourself into this group or to become the victim of a collective energy vampire.

Three "Yes" Responses

If you answered "yes" to all three questions, beware. The group spirit suffers from a drastic lack of energy and is thirsting for victims. You can protect yourself if you immediately start using the following emergency exercises, designed for cases like these.

TEN SIMPLE RULES TO PROTECT AGAINST A MOB ATTACK

First, ask yourself whether you wouldn't be better off at a different job. If you conclude that you do not want or cannot afford to leave your current position, try improving your situation as much as possible by following these ten rules.

> **FIRST MOB RULE**
>
> Intensify energy production.

Starting immediately, intensify your exercises for the production of energies (meditation, physical workouts) that you carry out at home in your safe area (see chapter 7). End your exercises each time with the exercise for the closing of the chakra.

> **SECOND MOB RULE**
>
> Strengthen your aura regularly.

Effective immediately, start carrying out exercises to strengthen your aura on a regular basis. Every morning before you go to work, shield your aura by programming your consciousness (see chapter 3).

> **THIRD MOB RULE**
>
> Shield and extend your aura.

During your morning exercises, visualize your guarded aura extending until it shields your physical work area (office, desk, or cubicle). End this additional visualization by imagining that your aura contracts again at the end of your day until it surrounds your body as tightly as usual.

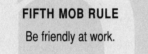

FOURTH MOB RULE

Cleanse your aura on a regular basis.

Start carrying out regular exercises to cleanse your aura immediately (see chapter 3). The best time for this would be at night, after coming home from work. Complement these exercises by cleansing your chakras (see chapter 5).

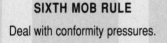

FIFTH MOB RULE

Be friendly at work.

Do not be reclusive or secluded at work, but try to be accessible and tolerant. At the same time, do not make any mention of your private life to members (active or latent) of the energy vampire group, especially not of your spiritual convictions or habits.

SIXTH MOB RULE

Deal with conformity pressures.

At work, accept all "unwritten laws" that you are not absolutely opposed to. The group may know anyway that you are "different" and not willing to conform entirely, but they will see that there are some items that you share in common. Still, refuse to conform on all points that you are strongly opposed to—in a friendly but decisive manner. For example, if there is a forced group consensus at your work that one should only drink tea—and, under no circumstances, coffee—and you are not a regular coffee drinker, then you should go along with that habit. On the other hand, if the group demands that everyone go to a hamburger joint for lunch and eat burgers, you should not feel the need to go if you are a vegetarian.

SEVENTH MOB RULE

Do the best work you can.

Once you have decided that you want to keep your job, you should—for your own good—make the best of it: if you invest a lot of energy in your work, you will get as much back, in the short or long term. Often the group will feel obliged to recognize your accomplishments, or at the very least, this effort at work will allow you to avoid being weakened, which would inevitably happen if you worked only grudgingly and without much care.

EIGHTH MOB RULE

Don't ponder negative group energies.

Try not to think about the negative energies that circulate among your group, or about what would happen if the group picked you as its next energy victim. Otherwise, you run the danger of creating just such energies within you—and thus attracting the attention of the group.

NINTH MOB RULE

Care for your energy sources outside of work.

Design your life in such a way that it includes sources for gaining new energies in your free time, even beyond your regular energy exercises. Make sure to spend time with family and friends and develop hobbies that reflect your needs and your personality.

TENTH MOB RULE

Protect yourself by loving your coworkers.

Whenever you feel someone at work being hostile or unfriendly toward you, concentrate on thoughts of altruistic love and empathy toward this person. Think about how and why this person deserves your empathy. Since you understand and are following the universal energy laws, you have an excess of life energy—and others attack you only because they lack this energy. Avoid any feeling of pity or arrogance, and allow part of your positive energies to flow to this person.

EXERCISE: DIFFUSING PSYCHIC ATTACKS WITH THE RUBBER WALL METHOD

One of the universal energy laws states that aggressive energies aimed at one by an attacker will return to their origin like a boomerang if they, for whatever reason, miss their target. We can use this law in the defense against energy vampires by training our aura to bounce back any attack.

Imagine that the outermost layer of your aura is made up of rubber. Much like a tense bow before an arrow is shot, your aura gives in until it is tight—only to fire back negative energies with the same power to their originator.

11

How to Protect Your Company against Energy Vampires

W e can view business enterprises in much the same way that we view human individuals—as energy-filled beings that soak up energies, transform them, and pass them on. The best-known symbol of these commercial energy flows is money, which we hope to "make" by opening and running a company. Before we do that, however, we have to invest energies in many different ways—ideas, capital, our own labor, and that of others. These energies are supposed to flow back at some point in the form of money and wealth. But it is not always just we who want to profit from our enterprise: companies are also potential victims of energy vampires, which try to take over the energies a business has accumulated.

What can we do against such a theft of energy? How can we defend against it? And how can we prevent it? If you want to protect your company against energy vampires, you will need to take certain precautions inside and outside of your business. Just as psychic garbage (see chapter 6) can accumulate in our subconscious and attract energy thieves, certain weak points of a company's structure and culture can also attract energy vampires. And just as our individual aura needs to be cared for, strengthened, and shielded to be able to defend itself against energy aggressors, a company, too, needs an external skin that has strong energies and tightly combines the separate parts. Such an external skin is the only defense against vampire attacks.

"SKELETONS IN THE CLOSET" ATTRACT ENERGY VAMPIRES

It is not always an unfounded rumor when people say of a successful businessperson that he or she buried bodies along the way to achieve success for his or her company. If later on you find out that this business-person fell ill, became destitute, or was hit by bad luck, you could conclude that the rumor contained more than just a grain of truth.

Usually, of course, these are not buried bodies in the criminal sense and no prosecutor will be investigating these "murders." Most often, these previously successful people who suddenly hit upon bad luck, accidents, or sickness simply stumbled over the dead energy bodies they buried beneath their company. No different from suppressed memories that can serve as magnets of misfortune among individuals, these dead bodies will have been blocking positive energies within the company for a long time and attracting negative energies outside the company. This will continue until at some point a critical mass is reached where the negative energies are greater than the positive ones—and the whole company suddenly comes crashing down. But those who are able to see and read energy balances will have long known that all was not well.

Some of the bodies that might be in a company's closet are as follows:

DUBIOUS FOUNDING CAPITAL: The company's founder used improper means to obtain the money to start the company. Such things tend to catch up with one later when the thief in turn is swindled by somebody else.

ABANDONED PARTNERS: Business partners who helped build the company are forced to leave before the company's big success. I know of several cases in which stellar careers suddenly came to an end after a hostile takeover. In each case, it later turned out that the "victim" had dealt no better with his own partners in years past.

EXPLOITATION OF IDEAS: Inventions, patents, or commercially advantageous concepts are marketed by a company, without rewarding the creator adequately for the success of the idea. The originator of the idea is often an employee of the company—companies such as this in turn frequently will fall prey to industrial espionage, attracted by the negative energy of the company's theft.

NEGLECT OF CERTAIN BUSINESS AREAS: Often, much more subtle "energy killings" will over time cause an avenger to appear. Internal imbalances of power, pay, and appreciation—perhaps between managers and creative forces in a company—can become magnets of misfortune, for example, when the company's creative department suddenly makes a catastrophic mistake.

In principle, energy balances and exchanges are no different at companies than with individuals. Among individuals, such exchanges happen between body, spirit, and soul; among companies, these exchanges are between different hierarchical levels, departments, and divisions—and also between the present and the past. Energy objects of any kind or size have a memory; they remember the past and attract those circumstances and people in the external world that respond to the internally stored information.

CASE STUDY: THE FORGOTTEN INVENTOR

When Burt F. showed up at my practice one summer and asked for my help as a spiritual energy and life counselor, I saw at first glance that he was close to complete physical and psychological exhaustion. His skin was gray and his aura had gray spots; yet he was only in his midforties and had until just a few months earlier been a dynamic, successful businessman, whose career, energy, and determination had been nationally lauded.

In his early years, Burt had founded a light-bulb factory, whose most advanced product, an energy-saving light bulb, soon generated headlines. It wasn't long before Burt, who had become known not only as the marketer of the product, but also as its inventor, had to expand his factory. Over the next few years, other production locations were added to the roster. In the mid-1980s, Burt F. seemed to have it made: he was a multimillionaire and the boss of a multinational company. All of the company's most successful products, however, were based on the energy-saving light bulb.

In the late 1980s the skies over the company's headquarters began to darken. No one could explain how this was possible, but suddenly throughout the country there emerged serious competitors, offering similar products of equal quality at lower prices. Burt's market share began to crumble, and his company's stock prices fell to the floor.

Burt had his legal department go after the competition, which he accused of copyright violations, illegal production of copyrighted materials, and brand-name infringement. Indeed, one of his competitors was pro-ducing a product with a name that was nearly identical to the brand name of Burt's light bulbs. In this altercation and some other disagreements, Burt's lawyers were able to score minor successes. The competition, however, remained: three competing companies took on Burt's com-pany and slowly but surely pushed it against the wall.

This continued until the lights were literally about to go out. Some of his production facilities had to close down, other restructuring measures loomed, and he was said to have already lost large chunks of his private fortune as well. He continued pursuing his competitors in never-ending legal battles, which ruined his and his company's public image. The media suddenly regarded Burt—who until just a few years ago had been an admired tycoon—as just a "bullying Goliath" against whom a num-ber of "brave Davids" dared to fight.

How to explain this dramatic turn for the worse? And, more impor-tant, what could still be done about it?

It was clear to me that this was a classic case of business energy vam-pires. Burt's competition was sucking energy from his company on a large scale. This energy was in the form of capital, image, confidence, and most of all, the plagiarized initial patent—the blueprint for the energy-saving light bulb.

I told Burt that I had a strong suspicion that somewhere in his com-pany's empire there was a magnet of misfortune, which had attracted the energy vampires of the external world. As he listened silently, I outlined the core spiritual energy concepts for him. Something or someone in his company had to have attracted the thieving rivals, since this is one of the basic energy laws.

"When you find yourself surrounded by a group of plagiarists," I explained, "an energy analysis suggests that there are some problems with your initial acquisition of the light bulb's patent as well."

For a long time, he looked at me with a fierce stare. I didn't push him. I had often seen how people suddenly remembered events that had long been forgotten. In my experience, this act of remembering in itself is an important step in the healing process, the way back to finding an energy balance. I saw how his expression slowly changed, to that of childlike amazement. It was as if he were listening to a voice inside him telling him things that caused overwhelming feelings of guilt. Suddenly, the tycoon moaned and hid his face in his hands.

When he finally looked up again, his voice was hesitant. Finally he said, "Dorothy, I have no idea how you could have known about this. I myself haven't even thought about it for many years. . . . It seems unbelievable now, but I never even thought about it at all anymore! I had just erased him from my memory—even though it was he . . . he, 'George the Genius,' as we called him . . . it was *his* invention! Oh my god, back then . . . I didn't steal his invention, but I bought this valuable invention for a lousy thousand dollars!"

The story he told me went as follows: Burt and George had studied engineering together. "George the Genius" had always been more talented in the technical realm, while Burt surpassed him in business sense and determination. Since George was constantly broke, he was happy that his friend bought the rights to the energy-saving light bulb for a thousand dollars. And while Burt was step by step building his first factory, George was stumbling along with his life, which was characterized by more ingenuous (though increasingly obscure) inventions, but mostly by women of dubious character and empty bottles of whiskey. Ten years later, Burt had made his first ten million dollars and had long lost track of his former friend. One day, George showed up at Burt's mansion, showing the traces of poverty and alcohol. The embarrassed tycoon gave the friend another five hundred dollars. After that he never saw George again and eventually forgot about him.

In the subsequent years, Burt made many more millions and was admired throughout the country. He surely had earned his fame, and just as surely, George by himself would never have been able to market his invention as effectively as had Burt. Nonetheless, when Burt allowed himself to be celebrated as the inventor of the product and later never tried to find his old friend to share his wealth with him—choosing, instead, to purge his friend from his memory and bury George in his subconscious—it resulted in bad luck not just for Burt, but for his company as a whole.

The company had been built on a suppressed injustice, like a castle on sand. It is little surprise, then, that his empire started to slide one day— and that it was those who were plagiarizing the light-bulb patent who were drawing Burt's company down. Equals attract. It was this energy law that had attracted energy vampires in the shape of idea thieves to Burt's empire, which was founded on a suppressed act of just such a theft.

"That is why, Burt," I concluded my diagnosis, "the energy vampires that are attacking your business can only be dealt with in one way: you have to find 'George the Genius' and pay a fair fee for his patent."

"How much?" he asked.

"Before these plagiarizers appeared," I responded, "you had a monopoly on the market for energy-saving light bulbs. You had 100 percent of the market share, correct? How much do you have today? How much did you lose to your competitors?"

"Forty percent."

"Then you know how much you should compensate George—or his relatives, if he is no longer alive."

"But this will ruin me!" exclaimed Burt. "First, these thieving competitors, and now I am supposed to pay George . . ." He stopped and looked at me with deep amazement. "So you think, Dorothy, that if I give George or his family his share, these thieves will disappear?"

I told him I was sure of it.

The rest of the story can be told very quickly. It took a few weeks until Burt was able to locate George, with the help of a private investigator. His former friend was living in a run-down housing project on the outskirts of a large city. In contrast to Burt, who had no children, George had seven.

There was an emotional reunion between these very different friends. At his own request, George received only a tiny share of the light-bulb empire that would not have been created had it not been for his genius. All other shares were transferred to his four ex-wives and his seven children.

Eight years have passed since Burt and George reconciled. In those years, Burt—to everyone's amazement—managed to bring down each of his three competitors. They were convicted of copyright infringement, and Burt regained the market for energy-saving light bulbs. Moreover, he now has the help of George's oldest son, who joined the company after finishing his engineering degree.

Burt proudly told me that George Jr. is a genius, too.

HOW TO CLEANSE YOUR COMPANY OF NEGATIVE ENERGIES

As the previous case study shows, companies have a "memory" that stores information about energy imbalances and blockages. If a company is headed by its founder or one of his or her children, or if it has for many years been led by a person who feels a deep connection with the company, there will be strong energy connections between this individual and the business: the aura of the founder and the aura of the company (see the following exercise) will in many cases be one and the same.

We also saw that the memory of a company can contain suppressed psychic garbage. This garbage can act as a magnet of misfortune, just as it does with individuals. Similarly, it is possible to cleanse the energy memory of an entity, such as a company, of negative energies with the use of some visualization exercises.

To do this, we once again go back to the golden fleece.

EXERCISE 1: CLEANSING YOUR BUSINESS WITH THE GOLDEN FLEECE

Think about which symbol best represents your business. This could be a logo, but also a different, less official symbol. In any case it should be an image, not words or numbers, in order to connect with the subconscious.

Now go to a place of your choice where you can comfortably lie down and won't be disturbed. For this exercise, lie down flat on your stomach and rest your arms along your sides, with your legs slightly spread.

Close your eyes and take a few slow and regular breaths until you can feel physical tension dissolving and your attention turning to the world inside you.

With your spiritual eye, visualize your personal happy place. At the center of this place is a golden fleece—soft sheep's or ram's wool with fibers of gold. You are lying on top of this fleece, on your stomach, with your head turned to the left or the right, whichever you prefer. Try to imagine as intensively as possible that all of your clothing and any skin not covered by clothes is covered with the symbol that represents your business.

Feel how warm and soft the golden fleece is. Use your spiritual eye to see the fleece's intense golden shine. Recognize that you are the embodiment of your business. Your subconscious contains all the memories that are stored in the memory of your business. Your feelings are the feelings of the energy entity that you founded or have led for many years.

Now feel how you are sinking deeper and deeper into the golden fleece. Observe how the fleece consists only of rays, light, and warmth. You are the company whose symbol covers your entire body. Your body and your head, which are sinking deeper and deeper into the golden fleece, are the body and head of the company whose symbol you are wearing. As you sink deeper and deeper into the fleece, the fleece slowly starts to float, a large, soft, and warming blanket of sheer energy.

The warm rays slowly start to penetrate you, and the fleece continues to float upward. In so doing, it passes through your body, cleansing your body's every cell, your soul's every fiber—and every chamber of your subconscious. Return to the knowledge that your body is the body of the company and your subconscious the mind of the company whose symbol is covering you from head to toe.

The golden fleece first passes through your external skin—your legs, chest and stomach, arms and neck, and the side of your face on which you sank into the fleece. The golden fleece slowly continues to float upward, and warmth overcomes you, a feeling of purity and love as the fleece continues to float upward.

While the golden fleece is passing through you, listen inside yourself for memories that are those of the company. If unpleasant, repressed memories emerge inside you, don't be afraid to spend a few moments with them. Once again feel the shock or frustration from back then, but also the calm with which you can say today: "In the end, I overcame it all." Or also, "This still has to be taken care of. But today I am strong enough and ready to do so."

The golden energy fleece cleanses your company of all old burdens, repressed memories, obstacles, old shadows, and weaknesses as it continues to float upward through your body.

Now the golden fleece emerges from your back and the back of your head and remains above your body for a moment. Your body is still covered with the symbol of your company. Observe the black toxins and dark spots that the golden fleece filtered from your subconscious. These are all the negative energies of which it cleansed your company.

The golden fleece takes all these dark spots with it as it continues to float upward, toward the sky. It will be cleansed in the infinite energy pool of the universe. Whenever you need it, it will be there for you—in all its shining purity and with its cleansing glow.

Ending the Exercise, Repetition

Remain at rest for a minute with your eyes still closed. Repeat several times, either out loud or to yourself:

> *"The memory of my company has been*
> *cleansed of all old toxins and spots.*
> *Only positive energies remain inside it.*
> *It is pure and free."*

Now open your eyes, take a few deep breaths, and slowly return to your normal state of consciousness.

Repeat this exercise as often as you feel is necessary.

Application in Real Life

If this exercise made you aware of repressed events or misfortunes, it may be necessary to resolve these in the external world. If, for example, you became aware that energy flows are divided unevenly within your company, that someone who did a lot for the company was passed over for a promotion, or that a person or department is not receiving enough appreciation or funds, you should fix these energy imbalances. Success will follow as it did in the previous example of the light-bulb tycoon, Burt F.

CLEANSE AND STRENGTHEN
THE AURA OF YOUR BUSINESS

Just as important as the processing and release of energy "dead bodies" in the internal world of your company is a strong, intact, and well-cared-for aura that will protect the company from outside attacks and represent your company's image to the world. However, an aura can be only as strong and complete as the business it surrounds. Thus, those who are able to see auras can read the true corporate identity of a business—including divisions or decline.

Once again, let us assume there is one person who is the founder of a company or has been at its helm for many years. This person will then represent this company to a very high degree. (This also applies to independent contractors or others running small businesses with only a few or no employees.) In many cases, charismatic individuals represent much larger companies, even multinational corporations with sales in the billions of dollars. Because of a deep connection between the company and this individual, and their close energetic relationship, they for the most part share an aura.

If you are the head of a company, there is a lot you can do to protect and strengthen your company simply by cleansing, strengthening, and shielding your personal aura on a regular basis.

Recommended Sequence of Exercises

Strengthen your aura in the pillar of light (see page 39).

Cleanse your aura (see page 43).

Cleanse your subconscious with the golden fleece (see page 83).

Cleanse your company with the golden fleece (see page 132).

Perform the following exercise for transferring your personal aura protection.

EXERCISE 2: TRANSFERRING YOUR PERSONAL AURA PROTECTION

Go to a quiet place where you won't be disturbed. The lights should be dimmed and any sound sources turned off. Sit or lie down in a comfortable position and close your eyes. Take a few slow and regular breaths until you feel your physical tension easing and your attention turning to the world inside you.

Make yourself aware of the way that your aura surrounds you as a colorful field of pulsating energy. Take a close look at your aura with your spiritual eye and touch it with your spiritual hands: your aura envelops your body as closely as a well-tailored suit of pure light.

With your spiritual eye, imagine that the different departments or divisions of your company correspond to different parts of your body. For example, in the case of a furniture store, the delivery department might correspond to your legs and feet, the production department to your upper body, arms, and hands, while management might be your heart and head, and so forth. Try to imagine these corresponding body parts as vividly as possible.

Now once again turn your attention to your strengthened and revitalized aura. It envelops your head and body, which represent the parts of your company. And just as your physical body forms a physical, spiritual, and energetic unit, all aspects of your company come together as an organic entity in which all energies flow freely and efficiently to all parts of the whole.

Visualization

Now take some deeper breaths and feel how with each breath you inhale your aura expands, and how it contracts with each breath you exhale. Your aura is like a second skin that surrounds you tightly.

Now turn your attention to your lower body and to the divisions of your company it represents. Feel how strongly and protectively your aura envelops these areas.

Repeat several times, either out loud or to yourself:

> *"[The name of the company division] is a part of my company, just like my legs and feet are a part of my body. My aura envelops and protects [name of division] as strongly as it envelops my feet and legs."*

Now turn your attention to the next part of your body that represents a part of your company in your visualization. Repeat the above affirmation.

Repeat these steps until you have arrived at the head—or the leadership—of your company.

If you want to protect your company even further, follow up this exercise by looking at the surface of your aura (the aura of your company). Watch how this clear surface starts to crystallize, like water that slowly turns to ice. Your aura is now as transparent as before, but no one can pass through it without your consent: you are inside an indestructible oval surrounded by crystals of light.

Repeat several times, either out loud or to yourself:

*"My aura envelops me and all aspects
of my company. Only positive energies can
pass through my shield."*

Ending the Exercise

Remain in your position for a few more minutes with your eyes closed and try to feel as intensively as possible that you embody your company, and that it, like yourself, is an integrated whole. Know that both you and your company are being protected by your aura.

Now open your eyes and slowly return to the external world.

PART FOUR:

Psychic Protection in Your Personal Life

I n this fourth part of the book, I cover our free time, in which we are still vulnerable to attacks by energy vampires—whether as consumers, or within our circle of friends and our private life—where we have substantially more control than at work over encounters with energy thieves. In the following chapters you will learn:

) How to protect yourself against energy vampires in society, whether they are pushy salespeople, pollsters, or others who constantly try to convince us of their views.

) How to shape your private relations with family, friends, and acquaintances in such a way that they are marked by a feeling of mutual respect and altruistic love, rather than by energy fights.

) How to change your relationship with your partner to ensure there is energetic harmony between the two of you. Or, if necessary, you can learn how to end a relationship with a "love vampire" if that person is not willing or able to make fundamental changes in the structure of energy flows in your partnership.

) How to change the structure and specifics of your lifestyle wherever necessary to ensure that negative energies are kept away. In this context, it may be a good idea to give up certain parts of your diet, media consumption habits, or even friends and acquaintances that have a negative effect on your energy balance.

Salespeople, Zealots, and Other Social Vampires

even in your free time you need to protect yourself from energy vampires. Some people seem to attract aggressive people. Whether they are pushy salespeople, telemarketers, or individuals trying to sell a certain political or religious view, they all jump on their victims with determination. And they seem to be able to pick out those among hundreds whose blood is especially welcoming. But why do some people seem predisposed to fall prey to these unpleasant people?

After reading the previous chapters in this book, readers will not be surprised if I suggest that, from my perspective, these problems have spiritual roots. In almost all the examples mentioned previously, we would find upon closer examination that the victims fell prey to attacks by energy vampires. Moreover, we would learn that this happened because they had certain subconscious expectations. Attracted by certain magnets of misfortune inside the victims, energy thieves were attracted and came running. This in turn leads us to conclude that in attacks of this kind, victims are not as *passive* and aggressors not as *active* as is commonly assumed. Both share a lack of awareness. In most cases, neither of the parties realizes that the supposed "sales discussion" or "consultation" is actually a fight for energy.

PROTECT YOURSELF AGAINST SUBLIMINAL MESSAGES AND INSISTENT SALESPEOPLE

Commercials for goods and services of every kind continue to become more refined in the way they try to stimulate our imagination and feelings. Commercials stimulate our need to own certain objects, to be "in," improve our image, or strengthen our self-confidence. At the same time, commercials appeal to all our fears—of isolation, rejection, embarrassment, and inferiority, as well as of old age and death. Although we can't overcome these fears by reading consumer self-help magazines, we can at least temporarily repress them.

This incessant flood of stimuli from commercials fills our subconscious with wishes and fears. These wishes and fears then attract their corresponding energy forces in the external world and draw us, like remote-controlled machines, straight to the stores. The salesperson pushing us to buy something is in fact only an embodiment of our commercial-influenced internal voice, which has started whispering, *"Buy this, and everyone will admire you!"* And if this voice is not enough to get us to buy the item, our internal voice, strengthened and projected to the external world in the form of the salesperson, will follow the wish with a fear: *"If you don't buy this, every-*

> Advertisements are often subtle energy fights.

one will think you can't afford it!" After this internally voiced threat (the fear of a lack of money is usually enough), the consumer in most sales pitches will give up: once again the vampire has sunk his teeth into the throat of the victim—to rob him or her of energy—in this case, symbolized by money.

SEVEN RULES FOR PSYCHIC SELF-PROTECTION IN THE CONSUMER WORLD

I propose the following seven rules to help guide us as consumers:

Reduce your passive consumption of advertising as far as possible. Don't allow yourself to be inundated by it. Try not to watch TV shows or listen

> **FIRST CONSUMER RULE**
> Avoid and ignore commercials.

to radio programs that are interrupted by commercials or turn off or mute the TV or radio as soon as commercials come on. In print media, flip past advertisements and ignore billboards on the streets.

Carry out exercises for the cleansing of your subconscious on a regular basis (see chapter 6). Pay special attention to cleansing yourself of images of desire that were created by advertisements.

> **SECOND CONSUMER RULE**
> Cleanse your subconscious on a regular basis.

Carry out exercises for the cleansing and strengthening of your aura on a regular basis (see chapter 3). While cleansing your aura, make sure you remove the energy junk that is the

> **THIRD CONSUMER RULE**
> Cleanse and strengthen your aura regularly.

result of commercials, advertisements, and sales pitches.

FOURTH CONSUMER RULE

Control your imagination.

Rein in your imagination and get used to consciously destroying images of desire for consumer goods. For example, visualize a certain desire being broken up by a hammer of light or a pistol that shoots rays.

FIFTH CONSUMER RULE

Get your information from reputable sources.

When you want to inform yourself about a product, get your information from reputable sources. Consult suitable sources, such as test results from consumer magazines, and form an opinion before you go to a sales outlet.

SIXTH CONSUMER RULE

Shield your aura before the sales pitch.

Before you talk to a salesperson, carry out the exercises for the strengthening and shielding for your aura (see chapter 3) several times. Also carry out the exercises for the cleansing and closing of the chakras (see chapter 5).

SEVENTH CONSUMER RULE

Beware of your feelings being manipulated during the sales pitch.

Never allow a salesperson to play on your wishes and fears. If he or she continues in an attempt to arouse your desire or guilt, end negotiations politely, but firmly.

PROTECT YOURSELF AGAINST OTHERS WHO COST YOU TIME AND NERVES

Pollsters or religious missionaries usually have the same trained eye for suitable victims that salespeople and telemarketers do. You might say that at least they are not after your money. But just as time is a symbol of energy over which we have control, the time and nerves that are required to repel pollsters or missionaries are also parts of our life energy we should not waste.

If you are among those who attract such annoying encounters, at some point you have surely asked yourself the following:

> How can I prevent these insistent people who preach on street corners from always wanting to explain to *me* that the world is about to end?

> How can I prevent these telephone pollsters from always bothering *me* with their fake interest and extensive questions?

> How can I prevent a friend or family member from always doubting my convictions or decisions?

Why do some people attract such annoying and insistent people while others never have to worry about them? By now, the answer should be obvious: something inside them attracts these people, just as light attracts moths. The "something" in these cases is a *lack of consciousness and self-confidence.*

In other words, when someone gives the impression of not having a strong sense of self, he or she will always attract swarms of people that strive to convince others of their personal views (political, religious, or whatever else). And, if someone gives the impression of letting the opinions of others—rather than their own internal compass—direct their actions, then he or she is the ideal victim for these pollsters, telemarketers, and so forth, who make a living of consumption based on the internal disorientation of others.

A lack of self-confidence attracts energy vampires.

If you are one of the people who have to deal with these nuisances on a regular basis, you will agree with me when I say that these people not only cost time and nerves, but also rob us of energy by forcing us to pay attention to them. In this manner, they create a one-way flow of energy that originates with us. They get high on our attention and on the power that they have over us. And although they pretend that they (and probably even believe themselves to) represent, for example, altruistic love, they are robbing us of our life energy.

What can we do to protect ourselves from energy bloodsucking of this unpleasant group? Here are my five golden rules:

Five Golden Rules to Protect Yourself from Vampire "Preachers"

FIRST PROTECTION RULE

Find your own issues.

Make yourself aware of which issues and topics are important to you, and which are of lesser or no importance. Using credible sources, inform yourself on the questions that matter to you, and reflect on them.

SECOND PROTECTION RULE

Meditate on existential questions.

Make a habit of meditating on existential questions and their meaning. Regardless of our education, we are all "experts" when it comes to the truly important questions in life. The answers that are right for you, you will find inside you.

THIRD PROTECTION RULE

Practice regular spiritual cleansing and strengthening.

Carry out regular exercises to cleanse your subconscious (see chapter 6) and to cleanse and strengthen your aura (see chapter 3). Also be sure to close your chakras after meditating or performing energy exercises (see chapter 5).

Talk to people whom you perceive as potential parasites or vampires only about issues on which you have your own, clearly established opin-

FOURTH PROTECTION RULE
Stand by your own opinion.

ion. Defend this opinion firmly, but politely. Any attempts to change your opinion will either not be undertaken in the first place or will cease quickly.

Design your circle of friends and acquaintances with an eye to your spiritual orientation. If necessary, stop your contact with people who continue to engage you in energy-

FIFTH PROTECTION RULE
Select friends and acquaintances consciously.

consuming arguments, or people who emit negative energies.

13

Protecting Your Family against Energy Vampires

by protection against energy vampires, I mean that if you are a mother or father, you should not only do everything you can to protect your child from energy thieves, but should also use all your strength to ensure that your child does not have to fight for his or her required life energy.

Luckily, over the past couple of years, society has been sensitized to the horrible attacks that are grouped under the legal term "sexual child abuse." But the abuse of children's energy in other forms starts much earlier. Because the aura of young children is not well developed, it can only offer sparse protection against energy thieves. It is the responsibility of all adults not to abuse the energy of children. Those who treat children like small idiots and tease them in order to feel strong and smart themselves are guilty of a violent attack. This also applies to those "guardians" who abuse their power by intimidating, lying to, or ignoring children, or punishing them by withdrawing their love. These are all measures that force children to fight for the energy they need for life. That is because parental love is the energy of life.

> # Parental love is the source of all life energy for children.

Small children, especially, have no other way to get life energy than from parental attention and love. If this source runs dry, these children are left with no choice but to use all means to steal attention elsewhere. Thus, neglected children are potential energy vampires.

CASE STUDY: WHEN YOUR CHILD IS AN ENERGY VAMPIRE

Sarah V. was seventeen years old when her desperate mother, Eve, accompanied her to my practice for spiritual energy and life consultations. As a little girl, Sarah was a lively, smart, and sensitive child. Later, however, she was unable to meet academic expectations in school and she did not get along with her classmates. She remained an outsider and over the years became highly introverted. Moreover, from the onset of puberty, Sarah had become very underweight, not far from anorexia.

To the shock of her mother, Sarah had started experimenting with drugs at age fourteen, and even though she stopped using drugs two years later, she did not find the way back to a constructive path. Over the past two years, Sarah had tried to commit suicide four times. Her last suicide attempt was accidentally caught just in time; only a few weeks had passed since that attempt when the two of them came to see me for the first time. After a series of frustrating therapy attempts with psychoanalysis and other therapies, Eve referred to me as "her last hope," while Sarah preferred to ignore me and sit in silence.

I quickly learned that Sarah's father, Steve, had left the family when Sarah was five years old. "Our relationship was superficial and exhausting," said Eve with a tone that betrayed her anger even twelve years after the divorce. "He was constantly spending money on himself and expecting me to share his hobbies and current interests. When I finally suggested—after years of marriage—that he might show an interest in my modest hobbies, we had our first fight." Things went downhill from there. Steve found an attentive listener and companion in a woman named Kate and decided to leave Eve and little Sarah. First with surprise, then with horror, Eve witnessed that after Steve left their home, Sarah started imitating the tyrannical behavior of her father. In a bossy tone, she constantly demanded expensive new toys from her mother and threw fits if she did not receive undivided attention. Eve constantly found herself struggling to comfort and entertain her daughter, only to be bossed around by the five-year-old, playing any game the little girl had decided on. One night, without even the trace of a smile, Sarah said to Eve, "If you don't do what I say, I'll leave you and you'll be alone."

Unfortunately, the tired and exhausted Eve misunderstood this childish strategy as a "decisive power struggle." Without a word, she turned her back to the child and left the apartment, returning only hours later. When she returned, it was late at night, and she found Sarah, pale, sitting on the floor in her room, offering no reaction to her mother's presence.

After I had heard these details from Eve, I made my first diagnosis: Sarah had experienced the decidedly negative situations that turn a person into an energy vampire.

> She had never experienced members of her family giving one another attention and love in a harmonious and balanced way.
> She had never learned that there were other ways to orient oneself than the material obsessions of her father.
> From observing her father, she had come to the conclusion that the only way to get life energy was to use emotional blackmail.

With the tyrannical method that she had learned from her father as a little child, she had continued to try to get the attention of her mother, as well as that of fellow students and teachers, by force. She had become dependant on this domination of others as the only way she knew to receive life energy. Whenever the strategy of threats and blackmail (her father's method) failed, Sarah was in a panic. How else would she in the future be able to get the life energy she needed?

Sarah found herself in the destructive company of drinkers and cocaine addicts when she was fourteen. The alcohol and cocaine were easily accessible energy sources for her, even if they offered only destructive energy. They also became an effective way to get Eve's attention: "Give me your love—or I will drink and drug myself to death," was her message. After becoming increasingly drawn into a world of negative energies, Sarah finally found the ultimate means of blackmailing Eve, and a solution to her energy problem: a half-calculated, half-serious game of suicide.

I am sure you will believe me when I say that it was long and hard work for me to lead Sarah onto her spiritual path and to accompany her on her first steps to health. First, I had to get Sarah to trust my concept of a "gentle creation of energy." I felt I had to do this during our first encounter, for I feared Sarah's suicidal tendencies had grown so strong that I might not get a second chance. I used the elite energy method that I discuss in chapter 4: I called up a feeling of loving Sarah with all my heart, completely and without any reservations. I then steered the flow of my energy toward Sarah, who was surprised by the sudden attention and supply of that pure energy for which she had been so desperately looking. In this way I convinced her that I knew of a way to free her of the fundamental problem of her existence. I then got her to carry out a program for the creation of energy through exercises and meditation. That was followed by exercises to cleanse the subconscious (chapter 6), as well as exercises for the cleansing and strengthening of the aura (see chapter 3).

At the same time, I was also helping Sarah's mother. The energy-exhausted Eve also learned to raise and stabilize her energy level. I then showed her how to protect herself against vampiric attacks from her daughter by strengthening and shielding her aura, and by consciously closing her chakras (see chapter 5). In this way, I prevented the two of them from falling back into their old vampire-victim pattern and thus strengthened Sarah on her spiritual path of reaching energy autonomy.

Of course, along the way we encountered many crises and frustrating setbacks. But that only deepened my joy and gratitude when Sarah told me, months later, "I made it, Dorothy. Without you I would have died of thirst like a traveler in the desert. Thank you." With these words, she gave me a warm smile full of love. This time it was I who felt the wave of energy flooding over me. No doubt, Sarah had learned her lesson.

FIVE RULES FOR THE SPIRITUAL REARING OF YOUR CHILD

There are a few rules for the spiritual rearing of children. If you follow these rules—and make sure that other people your children relate to do so as well—you will protect your children from two things: being the sad victim of energy vampires, and becoming energy vampires themselves.

> **FIRST PARENTING RULE**
> Encourage the natural sensory endowments of your child.

During the early years, practically every child has psychic qualities. This ability to see auras, or to "read" the feelings and thoughts of others, usually gets lost at age six or seven—but only if it is ignored or repressed. Thus, if your child reports so-called supernatural abilities to you, acts them out, or sketches them on paper, encourage those activities and affirm that you believe in the reality of these experiences.

Through meditation, physical exercises, visualizations, and rituals, you can provide a role model for your child and help the child understand the spiritual concept of universal energy, and the aura and its four dimensions.

> **SECOND PARENTING RULE**
> Perform meditation, physical exercises, visualizations, and rituals to connect with your higher self.

Think about your child with a feeling of deep and pure love as often as possible. At the same time, develop in your child a sense and readiness to strengthen others through attention and appreciation—in other words, by providing them with life energy.

> **THIRD PARENTING RULE**
> Give your child as much attention and life energy as you possibly can, especially during his or her first years of life.

You should spare your child anything that is harmful or unnecessary. Those things that are beneficial should play a large role in your child's life. From a spiritual perspective, the consumption of meat, for example, is harmful, since it dulls the senses. The same holds true for an excessive consumption of media, which disorients our consciousness and subconscious by flooding them with desires from the physical world. *Beneficial* means anything that encourages the creation of energies and a holistic development—which includes physical activity as well as creative games or performing music.

> **FOURTH PARENTING RULE**
> All principles of how to raise your child should derive from the central considerations of heightening the energy level, strengthening the aura, and encouraging the spiritual development of your child.

FIFTH PARENTING RULE

Make a habit of extending your aura protection to your child.

It is important to extend your aura to protect your child during his early years. I offer several exercises in this chapter to learn how to do this.

EXERCISE: EXTENDING YOUR AURA PROTECTION TO YOUR CHILD

Go to a quiet place where you won't be disturbed. Dim the lights and turn off any sources of noise. Sit or lie down in a comfortable position and close your eyes. Take a few slow and regular breaths until you can feel physical tension easing and your attention turning to the world inside you.

With your spiritual eye, imagine having your child close to you (on your arm or lying next to you).

Make yourself aware of how your aura surrounds you and your child as a colorful field of pulsating energy. Take a close look at your aura with your spiritual eye and touch it with your spiritual hands: your aura surrounds you and your child like an elastic cover of pure light.

Visualization: Inflating Your Aura

Now take a few deeper breaths and feel how your aura extends with every breath you take. With every exhalation, it becomes more and more inflated, like a balloon you are filling with your breath. Feel how your aura is changing shape the farther away it is from the contours of your body and of your child.

Keep breathing air into your aura until it has the shape

of a large egg. You and your child are now inside a large oval of white light.

Repeat several times, either out loud or to yourself:

"My child and I are guarded against any
psychic attacks—only positive energies
can penetrate our guard."

Repeat this affirmation until you are completely sure that your energy guard is reliably protecting you and your child.

If you feel the need to further protect yourself and your child, look closely at the surface of the aura and watch as its smooth surface starts to crystallize, like water turning to ice. Your aura is now as transparent as it was before, but no one can pass through it anymore without your consent: your child and you are in an indestructible oval of crystal light.

CLEANSING AND BANNING RITUAL TO GUARD YOUR HOME AGAINST ENERGY VAMPIRES

In a fashion similar to how we extend our aura protection to our company (see chapter 11) or create a spiritual safe area (see chapter 7), we can also safeguard our family home against attacks by energy vampires. The following ritual serves to symbolically cleanse your home of negative energies and to ensure the protection of positive energies. The symbolic cleansing will also render your home off-limits to energy vampires: because it will not contain negative energies after its cleansing, it will no longer attract energy thieves.

As parents, you should carry out this ritual together with your children, if possible. When shared with all family members, this ritual strengthens harmony and cohesion within the family. Children are easily excited about symbolic and visual acts and usually intuitively grasp the deeper meaning behind them.

This ritual can be carried out when moving into a new home, but also in a home where you have lived for some time. It will cleanse the home of negative energies and guard it against energy thieves.

Preparation

For the banning and cleansing ritual, you will once again need symbolic representations of the five magical elements:

> A bowl with salt or bread crumbs to represent the element Earth
> A bowl with water to represent the magical element Water.
> A white wax candle to symbolize the element Fire
> A bowl with incense to represent the element Air
> A glass ball to represent the element Spirit

Make sure, depending on the size of your house and the number of rooms, that the bowls and candle are large enough.

Discussion and Distribution of Roles

Give yourself plenty of time to prepare this ritual. Talk with your children about each of the magical elements, their powers and significance. If your family consists of five people (parents and three children, or a different configuration), it is highly recommended that each of the five elements be "embodied" by a different family member.

In this case, you should discuss the distribution of the roles with your children beforehand. Who in the family is—based on their character, temperament, likes, and dislikes—especially well suited to embody the element Earth? Who is predestined for the elements Water, Fire, and so forth?

WHICH ELEMENT FITS EACH FAMILY MEMBER?

The higher elements of Air and Spirit should usually be embodied by the parents (and, if the grandparents live in the home, by them as well). Therefore, you should distribute the elements Earth, Water, and Fire among the children where possible. The elements are not gender specific and either sex may represent any of the elements.

- The element Earth suits personalities who are "grounded," those who are closely connected to nature, possess calm dispositions, and tend toward quiet confidence.
- Empathic, affectionate dreamers are well suited to the element Water.
- The element Fire is associated with strong-willed, active personalities.
- The element Air most corresponds to an adult (or notably mature younger person) whose thoughts and actions are characterized by rational and conscious decisions.
- The element Spirit is typically embodied by an adult (or notably mature younger person) whose actions, thoughts, and feelings are characterized by a high degree of idealism and spirituality.

For the ritual itself, each "embodiment" of each of the five elements will walk through the whole house to symbolically clean each room in a predetermined order. If your family consists of more than five people, the family should collectively decide ahead of time which people will represent which elements; the other family members will observe the ritual with full concentration. If the family consists of fewer than five members, family members may take on more than one role in the ritual.

For simplicity, I will use as an example a family of five.

Beginning the Ritual: The Cross of Elements

Ask all five family members to go outside the main door of the house that you want to cleanse of energy pollutants. Each of the five family members carries the symbolic representation of the element that person embodies in his or her right hand. Position all family members, including yourself, in the shape of a cross outside your door as shown in figure 6. (In families with fewer than five people, those family members representing more than one element may set the symbolic representation of one of the elements in place while standing in the position of the other element.)

The first family member to enter the house is the one who embodies the element Earth. That individual is followed by Water, then Fire, then Air, then Spirit (family members representing more than one element may carry the symbolic representation of those elements into the house together, while remaining in the position of one of those elements). Go to the first room that is to be cleansed. It is important to re-form the cross formation upon entering the room to be cleansed. All should close their eyes and take five deep and regular breaths.

Calling the Element Earth

Once in the room to be cleansed, the embodiments of the elements Water, Fire, Air, and Spirit should say loudly and solemnly:

> *"Element earth, we request your protection*
> *for this room."*

Now all open their eyes. With slow, solemn steps the embodiment of the element Earth walks along the edge of the room in a clockwise circle. While doing so, this person holds the bowl with the symbolic bread crumbs or salt in the right hand and uses the left hand to disperse a little of the bread or salt representing Earth along the border of the room five times.

While this is happening, the embodiments of the other elements remain still and repeat the following each time the element Earth is dispersed:

> *"The element Earth protects and*
> *cleanses this room."*

After the embodiment of the element Earth has finished walking the room in a circle, he or she returns to Earth's position in the cross for-

Figure 6. Cross formation of the family and their corresponding magical elements

mation. Now the embodiments of the four other elements say loudly and solemnly:

> *"Element Earth, we thank you for your*
> *protection and for cleansing this room."*

Now all close their eyes and take five deep breaths.

Calling the Element Water

Now the embodiments of the elements Earth, Fire, Air, and Spirit say loudly and solemnly:

"Element Water, we request your
protection for this room."

Now all open their eyes. With slow, solemn steps the embodiment of
the element Water walks along the edge of the room in a clockwise circle. While doing so, this individual carefully holds the bowl of water in
his or her right hand and uses the left hand to disperse a few drops of the
water along the border of the room five times.

While this occurs, the embodiments of the other elements remain still
and repeat the following each time the element Water is dispersed:

"The element Water protects and
cleanses this room."

After the embodiment of the element Water has finished walking a circle
circle, he or she returns to Water's place in the cross formation. Now the
embodiments of the four other elements say loudly and solemnly:

"Element Water, we thank you for your
protection and for cleansing this room."

Now all close their eyes and take five deep breaths.

Calling the Element Fire

Now the embodiments of the elements Earth, Water, Air, and Spirit say
loudly and solemnly:

"Element Fire, we request your
protection for this room."

Now all open their eyes. The embodiment of the element Fire lights
the white candle. With slow, solemn steps, that person walks along the
edge of the room in a clockwise circle while waving the candle five times
in regular intervals, imagining that some sparks fly toward the edge of
the room.

While this is happening, the embodiments of the other elements remain still and repeat the following with each rotating wave as the sparks of the element Fire are released:

"The element Fire protects and
cleanses this room."

After the embodiment of the element Fire has finished walking the circle, he or she returns to Fire's place in the cross formation (the candle is not extinguished). Now the embodiments of the four other elements say loudly and solemnly:

"Element Fire, we thank you for your protection
and for cleansing this room."

Now all close their eyes and take five deep breaths.

Calling the Element Air

Now the embodiments of the elements Earth, Water, Fire, and Spirit say loudly and solemnly:

"Element Air, we request your
protection for this room."

Now all open their eyes, and the embodiment of the element Air lights the incense he or she carries in the right hand. With slow, ceremonial steps the embodiment of the element Air walks along the edge of the room in a clockwise circle while shaking the bowl with incense being carried in the right hand in five regular intervals, so that some smoke wafts along the edge of the room.

While this occurs, the embodiments of the other elements remain still and repeat the following each time the element Air is dispersed:

"The element Air protects and
cleanses this room."

After the embodiment of the element Air has finished walking the circle, he or she returns to Air's position in the cross formation (the incense is not extinguished). Now the embodiments of the four other elements say loudly and solemnly:

> *"Element Air, we thank you for your protection*
> *and for cleansing this room."*

Now all close their eyes and take five deep breaths.

Calling the Element Spirit

Finally, the embodiments of the elements Earth, Water, Fire, and Air say loudly and solemnly:

> *"Element Spirit, we request your*
> *protection for this room."*

Once again all open their eyes and the embodiment of the element Spirit lifts his or her right arm to the height of the head, so that everyone can see the glass ball that person holds. With slow, ceremonial steps the embodiment of the element Spirit walks along the edge of the room in a clockwise circle while lifting the right hand, and holding the glass ball upward, as high as possible. While this is happening, the embodiments of the other four elements say loudly and solemnly:

> *"See how the spirit shines. See how the shining*
> *ball extends and how it fills the room with energy.*
> *Feel the warmth and purity of the element Spirit*
> *that fills this room with positive energy."*

After the embodiment of the element Spirit has finished walking the circle, he or she returns to Spirit's place in the cross formation, holding the ball at chest level. Now the embodiments of the four other elements say loudly and solemnly:

> *"Element Spirit, we thank you for your*
> *protection and for cleansing this room."*

Now all close their eyes and take five deep breaths.

Ending the Ritual

Carry out this banning and cleansing ritual in every room to be cleansed of energy pollutants.

After finishing the ritual, return to your starting points at the door. Make sure to remain in cross formation. All five family members should lift up their right arms, holding their symbolic representations of the elements, and say with conviction:

> *"Our home has now been cleansed and is safe.*
> *Only positive energies can enter it."*

It is usually necessary to perform this ritual only once, when you first move into a new home.

14

Protection against Energy Struggles in Love and Marriage

In previous chapters, we touched on this delicate topic at several points: what can we do if we realize that the person at our side is an energy vampire? Such relationships are much more prevalent than one might think. It is no surprise, since nothing gives us a more reliable access to a person's life energy than that person's *love*, which literally floods us with energy.

THE THREE BASIC TYPES OF RELATIONSHIP VAMPIRES

In the realm of relationship vampires, we can differentiate between three basic types:

❐ The charismatic love hunter
❐ The parasitic homebody
❐ The energy beggar

The Charismatic Love Hunter

This hunter is usually a man, but sometimes appears as a woman, too. He is the type of man that gets women: his look is as sharp as a vampire's tooth, and his charisma resembles a wave that knocks over its victims. No wonder that the objects of his affection are usually dizzied: the ringing in their ears is the sound of their life energy being transferred to him. This is the character we often think of as the "love 'em and leave 'em" type, the "ladies' man," or, inversely, his female equivalent.

Even when people suspect they might have fallen for a love-hunting energy vampire, most victims are too weak to defend themselves. Victims of these hunters frequently let themselves be sucked of life energy for weeks or months, all the while saying to themselves or their friends, "I know he's bad news, but I just can't stay away!" Moreover, it is usually not the victim who finds the strength to rid herself of the vampire, but the vampire that goes looking for the next victim—one who has a full energy level. Sometimes a friend or family member may also drive the vampire away.

The Parasitic Homebody

This type of relationship vampire can be a man or a woman. In contrast to the charismatic hunter, this type of vampire is not looking for a sudden, overwhelming attack and complete exhaustion of his victim. Instead, the parasitic homebody prefers a long-term connection with a victim which allows the vampire to suck the energy from the peaceful setting of home. While the energy hunter resembles a binge drinker, the long-term parasite is more of a functioning alcoholic, who avoids the full-fledged high and takes care of his energy source so it will serve him longer.

The suffering of victims of this kind of vampire often lasts for many decades—sometimes throughout a marriage. Typically, the parasitic home-body is introverted, but possesses a tyrannical side. This individual has a tendency toward self-pity and is often bad tempered and slightly depressed. In this way, the parasitic homebody forces the affection of his or her partner, who gives up energy by trying to cheer up or console the parasite. This vampire is weakened in the absence of an energy source, but comes alive when he or she can once again sink teeth into a victim's throat.

If, in a long-standing marriage, one partner passes away soon after the other, the reason for this may not always stem from a "broken heart." Rather, it may represent the end of a long-term parasite who is unable to find another source of energy.

The Energy Beggar

I must warn of the dangers of the energy vampirism that can occur during the illnesses—often chronic—of a partner. It is certainly not my intention to suggest that sick people are inherently energy vampires. Yet the stress and pain that naturally accompanies illness can quickly open the way to fear and struggles for life energy.

In the long run, nobody has the strength for two. Of course, the healthy partner can and should try to hold the center of strength for both partners in the face of physical illness. But when one of the partners is chronically ill—or if there is a large age difference of twenty years or more between them—the healthy partner at some point will not be able to keep supplying the necessary strength. The caretaker will be exhausted of energy and will eventually fall sick as well, perhaps suffering a nervous breakdown.

If both partners are aware of this danger ahead of time, and if they carry out spiritual exercises (such as meditation or yoga, or physical exercises) in combination with a healthy diet (see chapter 15) to replenish their energy supplies, they are usually able to deal with the energy problems that a long-term illness poses for a relationship. In such cases, the danger that the ill partner will consciously or subconsciously turn into an energy vampire is low: that person will have the means, though limited, to generate energy; the healthy partner will have more energy than others, because of her spiritual exercises, and will thus be able to supply the ill partner with energy for far longer than others could.

However, things get more complicated when partners in such a relationship are not aware of these dangers. In those cases, it is nearly inevitable that the sick partner will try to boost falling energy levels at the expense of the other partner. The healthy partner will almost inevitably be blackmailed into staying in the relationship in solidarity, which, in the long term, will undermine that person's own vitality. There are also many cases where illnesses without a clear physical cause are an expression of an energy deficit. This is especially true for illnesses with symptoms that are difficult to substantiate (e.g., hypochondria, some types of headaches, and some types of depression). With a healthy partner's attention (and energy), the symptoms will disappear and the energy beggar's condition will improve— only to return in full force once this energy source gets cut off again.

The weapon that the energy beggar uses to fulfill his or her demands is usually pity, a form of blackmailing through guilt. The sympathetic partner pays a blackmail "debt" through self-sacrifice. This is different from the sometimes exhausting but healthy exchange of loving support, in that the caregiver is unable to determine or choose how and when support is given. The fact that these energy transactions in the relationship usually take place subconsciously makes it even more difficult for either partner to see what is going on.

HOW TO TAME THE ENERGY VAMPIRE AT YOUR SIDE

Energy fights of any of the three types outlined here are not helpful to either partner. It is clear why they are not good for the victim, but the thieves, too, ultimately cannot be happy with their situation. Whether they are charismatic love hunters, parasitic homebodies, or energy beggars, they always remain dependent on their partner's energies, which they do not control, and without which they could exist only in a limited way—or not at all. What then can we do to free ourselves of these energy vampires?

Should you one day realize that your partner is taking your energies, there are some basic questions you will have to ask yourself.

Questions for the Victims of Relationship Vampires

❯ Do you still love your partner, despite knowing that he or she is an energy vampire?

❯ Do you want to end this relationship?

❯ Do you want to try to change this relationship so fundamentally that the energy attacks by your partner become unnecessary? If so, will your partner be ready and able to overcome his or her previous vampiric behavior?

If you answered "no" to the first question, the following points will not be of much interest. In this case, I suggest looking at the energy-building exercises in earlier sections of this book to build and maintain your energy resources while you take active steps to end the relationship. Those, however, who find that they cannot or do not wish to part with their beloved energy vampire—despite the suffering they have gone through and the risks in staying with him or her—are about to enter an adventure of a special kind in attempting to tame the vampire.

THREE RULES FOR PROTECTION AGAINST ENERGY VAMPIRES

If you and your partner have decided to stay together and to fundamentally change your relationship, you should absolutely observe the three rules that follow.

FIRST RELATIONSHIP RULE

Neither of the partners can be permanently dependent on the other's energy.

The first rule does not say that you should no longer support one another. It does mean, however, that under the majority of circumstances, each partner in a relationship has to be able to survive on his or her own. There are some basic practical steps that you can take to ensure this:

- Both partners should practice spiritual exercises for the creation of energy on a regular basis.
- If you initially still doubt the "energy trustworthiness" of your ex-vampire, don't hesitate to retreat to a personal safe area for meditation and other spiritual exercises.
- If necessary, you and your partner should do everything possible to increase the relationship energy level and to give up anything that might make the relationship lose energy. This may, for example, include giving up the consumption of drugs.
- If your partner is dependent on energy transfers from you for health reasons, you should not deny him or her your support. But you should make sure that your partner also gets additional energy from sources other than you (friends, relatives, or professional helpers). You alone would be overwhelmed if you had to function as a permanent energy station.

In almost every relationship, one person will have more energy and vitality than the other. This can be very clear, or reflect a more subtle difference in energy. And by energy balance, I do

> **SECOND RELATIONSHIP RULE**
> There has to be an energy balance between both partners.

not mean a static equality, but rather dynamic harmony: when two people can develop and express their strongest talents, interests, and needs in a relationship, no one partner will continuously be dominant in energy. Rather, this dominance will switch back and forth between the two, depending on which abilities and interests are in the foreground at the moment. Use the following recommendations to assist yourself in developing a balanced energy relationship with your partner:

- Using meditation, try to identify your strongest talents and

most vital needs. Now meditate to identify the talents and
needs of your partner.

❍ Ask yourself during this meditation what you expect of your
relationship and your partner in this life.

❍ Ask your partner to do the same, and exchange your thoughts
after the meditation. Do this on a regular basis. This will help
you build a deeper mutual understanding of each other's
strengths and expectations—and of the possibilities for both of
you.

❍ If your partner consistently generates less energy than you for
health reasons, there is a danger that both of you will end up
with a lower energy level. To counteract this effect, make sure
that, aside from your relationship, you are friends with people
whose energy levels correspond to yours more closely.

THIRD RULE
Energies between the partners have to
flow freely in the relationship.

The third rule stipulates that both
partners are truly ready and able to
respect not only their own interests
and talents, but also those of their
partner—for their own good, that
of their partner, and that of their relationship. It seems like common
sense that functioning relationships require mutual respect and love—
and indeed, this is at the core of energy patterns in every relationship. If
both partners steer their energies—in the form of attention or support—
on one point of common interest, this creates a free flow of energy that
allows both partners an optimal development and strengthens the relationship between them. For this to work, it is important that the point
of interest switch between the primary interests of the two partners. To
achieve this, I recommend the following steps:

❍ Together with your partner, practice the conscious directing of
your energies. Tune in to your partner's energy. When you feel
(and your sense for this will quickly become more attuned)

that the "moment" of the other has come—a moment (of any length) in which an internal potential of your partner wants to come out—direct your energies to your partner and concentrate on sending him or her feelings of encouragement, trust, strength, appreciation, and deep love. Communicate your needs so that your partner may do the same for you. Both of you will soon notice how helpful this controlled flow of energy is for the creative development of each of you as well as for harmonious connection in your relationship.

⤳ Every once in a while, check (not in a skeptical manner, but with a trusting eye) what kind of energy wonders the two of you can produce in this fashion. At the right moment, each of you now has access to a "turbo charger"—your own partner, who willingly puts his or her energies at your disposal because (and as long as) your partner can be sure that you will do the same.

15

A Long-Term Program to Reduce Stress and Energy Deficits in Modern Society

the demand for spiritual energy and life consulting has steadily grown in the past fifteen
years. It appears that in wealthy Western countries, fewer
and fewer people suffer from a lack of material goods. At
the same time, more and more people suffer from a lack of
energy.

There are many factors in the everyday lives of Western
people today whose effects add up to what I call a sort of

hyper-personal energy vampirism. Some of these factors are well known and are as follows:

- Bad diet in the age of junk food
- Detached and harried urban lifestyles
- Overstimulation of the senses by excessive media exposure and advertising

There is little sense in lamenting about today's culture and society or in crying about the lobbying power of the meat industry, the forces of corporate competition, or the multitude of audio and visual stimuli as if we were helpless victims. We are at least partly in control of whether we give in to these temptations or not. We have to go one step beyond recognizing the forces around us and say: "If we listen to the voice inside our heads and follow the path on which our higher self wants to lead us, we can be free of temptations and obligations that we do not want."

In other words, it is we who have attracted the people and situations in the external world that determine our lives today. We've done so with energies sent out by our subconscious. This in turn means that once we have cleaned up what is inside us and have removed negative energies from our subconscious, these energy vampire situations will, for the most part, disappear from our lives. But to be able to hear that voice inside of us, we cannot hesitate to reorient our lifestyles decisively and to remove external factors that draw energy from us. At the same time, we should do everything we can to make sure that in the future we will not be attracting or be attracted to such negative energies in the first place.

> **Internal negative energies attract energy-consuming lifestyles.**

SEVEN RECOMMENDATIONS TO PROTECT YOURSELF AGAINST HYPER-PERSONAL ENERGY VAMPIRISM

To make this practical and spiritual reorientation easier for you, I have summarized the most important rules and measures to prevent this hyper-personal energy vampirism in the following seven recommendations.

FIRST RECOMMENDATION

Choose a vegetarian diet.

Switch to a plant-based diet, preferably starting immediately. Meat, especially that of lower quality, can be cheaper than a vegetarian diet and easier to prepare. Beyond that, however, there is nothing to recommend it; meat pollutes with the negative energies of the animals that have been killed and processed for food.

EATING MEAT FIXATES US ON THE MATERIAL LEVEL
Because of the similarity between meat fibers (especially pork) and those of our own body, a diet with meat anchors us on the material level and in this way blocks the development of our spiritual consciousness.

PLANTS EMIT HIGHER-FREQUENCY ENERGY
In contrast, plants emit energy in higher frequencies than do the bodies of animals or humans. Thus, people who eat a vegetarian diet create a nutritional bridge between their material level and the fine-substance dimension.

EATING MEAT SUPPRESSES THE REALITY OF SLAUGHTERHOUSES
Moreover, a meat diet is closely connected with the foul-smelling energy of suppression. In case you are not exactly sure what I mean by this, I invite you to visit a slaughterhouse. A meat eater is part of a societal repression in which energy effects are no different from the psychic garbage we have in our subconscious—thus one who eats meat also shares in the negative energies this attracts in the external world.

VEGETARIANS ARE MORE SENSITIVE

On the other hand, if you switch to a vegetarian diet and eat fresh fruits and vegetables on a regular basis, you will find after just a few weeks a new sensitivity inside you that was previously dulled by eating meat. Some people initially find this newly awakened sensitivity irritating. But soon you will see how much larger and richer your world, your experience of your surroundings, and you yourself have become by forgoing the consumption of meat.

A PLANT-BASED DIET INCREASES YOUR ENERGY LEVEL

Most of all, however, you will notice how much a vegetarian diet will increase your energy level. Never again will you feel tired and heavy after a meal; instead, you will feel energized and light. In fact, after eating some quantities of meat, the human aura starts to weaken and even exhibit gray spots, while a plant-based meal will allow the aura to shine in strong and brilliant colors.

Free the energy that is in your food. Chew every bite thirty times before swallowing it. In this way, you will release the maximum energy that is contained in your food. While you

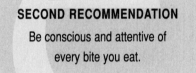

SECOND RECOMMENDATION
Be conscious and attentive of every bite you eat.

are eating, consciously think of the food you are eating until it transforms into energy inside of you.

CALL UP GRATITUDE AND LOVE WHILE EATING

While you are eating, try to call up a feeling of thorough gratitude and love for this world that provides you with such precious food. In this way, you will establish the connection with the cosmic energy pool, which is now providing your fine-substance dimension with the spiritual energy it needs.

AVOID EXCESS

Never eat too much and avoid eating sweets before meals. Excess of energy that is caused by too much food causes unwanted excesses in the outside world as well—disorder, chaos, unpleasant surprises.

FRUSTRATED EATERS PRODUCE NEGATIVE ENERGIES

Moreover, eating because you are frustrated is nothing but another mechanism of repression. The unpleasant feelings or memories that you are trying to repress by eating not only turn into extra pounds on your body, but also remain in your subconscious as psychic garbage, from where they—as negative energies—attract negative energies in the outside world.

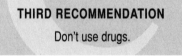

THIRD RECOMMENDATION

Don't use drugs.

Alcohol, nicotine, caffeine, chemical prescription drugs, and all other drugs are taboo. Although drugs do generate energies, the energies they generate are negative and are destructive to you and those around you.

DRUGS PAVE THE WAY FOR AN ENERGY DEFICIT

Dulling one's feelings and fleeing into an artificial world of dreams and feelings that is provided by alcohol, pharmaceuticals, or illegal drugs are among the surest ways of creating an energy deficit and energy vampirism—whether passive or active, as exhausted victim, or as perpetrator who steals those energies of others that he or she is no longer able to generate.

Refrain from these vices—if necessary, by seeking professional help. You will be surprised and happy to see how much more alive you will soon feel. The world around you will shine and glow in a way you might not have seen in years. The same, by the way, applies to the auras of former addicts, whose shine after successful treatment undergoes a remarkable transformation.

Those who watch too much TV harm themselves. The TV consumer alone is at fault for watching too much: nothing and no one can force you to spend your evenings, week-

ends, or the whole day with this junk box of sound and images. The following two important considerations against passive and unconscious TV consumption might strengthen you in the fight against this harmful habit.

WATCHING TV SWAMPS US WITH VISUAL STEREOTYPES

Our imagination is one of the most important instruments in developing and directing our consciousness. It is an invaluable tool in navigating our way through the world. When we allow our imagination to be flooded by images from dozens of TV channels, we have little chance of finding our own images, and even less chance of making them effective in a world that has been filled with foreign images.

MOST TV IMAGES ARE NEGATIVE ENERGIES

The overwhelming majority of images broadcast on TV—news reports on wars and other catastrophes, horror movies, and murder scenes—are nothing but visualized *negative energies*. Why in the world would we want to fill our inside world day in and day out with such energies? It is the same as eating food every day that we know is bad for us.

There is nothing wrong with watching TV from time to time, perhaps to see a movie or a report on a subject in which one is interested. But this habit can be moderated with responsible, self-nurturing choices. When considering "vegging" out in front of TV, ask yourself, "Am I comfortable with my choice to spend this time taking in media? Do I feel good about the source of this information and imagery that I am feeding my consciousness?"

FIFTH RECOMMENDATION
Watch your news "diet."

Just as the food we feed ourselves needs a combination of colors, flavors, and nutrients to represent a balanced diet, it is important for news to have a combination of local and global events representing many viewpoints.

Daily catastrophe consumption is similar to a flavorless diet. Too much consumption of negative news can damage the spirit and prevent individuals from having the energy to help heal and prevent those very catastrophes. Keeping in touch with the rest of the physical world through news is an essential part of participating in community. Yet, the innumerable daily reports of war, catastrophes, and accidents from around the world are a veritable shower of negative energies raining down upon us. Death and suffering are a part of life—as are births, seasons, joy, accomplishments, ideas, and creative expression. Make sure your news diet includes the items that feed your soul as well as your mind.

AVOID COMMERCIALIZED NEWS
Avoid being informed about current events through commercialized news programs or tabloids. Often the excessive presentation of great misery—the close-up images of corpses, starving people, refugees, the dying, and the ill—is linked to the energy of profit rather than the energy of compassion. As a result, we become desensitized and numb to the very real human suffering of others while simultaneously being overwhelmed by the constant message: Death and dying are all around!

INFORMATIVE WEEKLY OR MONTHLY REVIEWS ARE PREFERABLE
Certain radio stations and serious magazines (most recently, certain Internet services as well) instead offer weekly or monthly reviews. They don't offer the hectic "live" reporting and screaming headlines. Get used to being informed via these mediums, which can do without putting catastrophes in a commercial light. Therefore you can stay informed

about truly important political events while forgoing the consumption, and the exhausting effects, of daily commercial news.

One source of strain for body, mind, and soul that is still underestimated is the pollution of our highly technical world by so-called electrical smog.

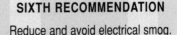

SIXTH RECOMMENDATION
Reduce and avoid electrical smog.

This electromagnetic junk can damage our organism on many levels, cause a variety of illnesses, and draw on the energies of people that are exposed to it for extended periods of time.

At home you should avoid using electrical appliances wherever possible. Microwaves are especially harmful; avoid using microwave ovens as well as cell phones, which have frequencies very close to those of radar. Inform yourself at local initiatives against electrical smog or by reading books on how to make your home and work safer.

Keep developing your consciousness to be aware of the fact that everything you have experienced in your life and will experience in the future represents energies that you either

SEVENTH RECOMMENDATION
Steadily develop your energy consciousness.

sent out or attracted. This applies to every experience you ever had, every person you have met, and every thought, image, feeling, memory, and idea that you are dealing with. When observing your energy, ask yourself the following questions:

➤ **Do I want to send out this energy?** If no, free yourself of it by cleansing your subconscious (see chapter 6). If yes, send it out consciously and look out for energy reactions that it provokes.

➤ **Do I want to receive this energy?** If no, shield yourself against it by strengthening your aura, as described in chapter 3. If yes, let it inside you consciously, and pay attention to the energy flow you return to its sender (whichever form it may take). Energetically harmonious relationships are characterized by the energy total of all participants being equal—and by the fact that the relationship continuously helps your individual energy level, as well as that of the group, keep rising.

I hope that you are able to build and strengthen your personal connection to the cosmic energies. After all, those who have made contact with their higher self will never again have to fight for life energy—the energy that is available in infinite amounts on the spiritual level.

Appendix
Directory of
Exercises and Rituals

EXERCISES TO SEE AURAS

EXERCISES TO STRENGTHEN AND CLEANSE THE AURA

CHAKRA EXERCISES

EXERCISES TO CLEANSE THE SUBCONSCIOUS

EXERCISES AND RITUALS FOR CREATING THE SPIRITUAL SAFE AREA

EXERCISES FOR PROTECTION AGAINST ENERGY VAMPIRES IN BUSINESS AND AT THE WORKPLACE

EXERCISE AND RITUAL FOR PROTECTION AGAINST ENERGY VAMPIRES IN YOUR PERSONAL LIFE AND FOR YOUR FAMILY

BOOKS OF RELATED INTEREST

Entity Possession
Freeing the Energy Body of Negative Influences
by Samuel Sagan, M.D.

Transforming Your Dragons
How to Turn Fear Patterns into Personal Power
by José Stevens, Ph.D.

Awakening the Energy Body
From Shamanism to Bioenergetics
by Kenneth Smith

Walking Your Blues Away
How to Heal the Mind and Create Emotional Well-Being
by Thom Hartmann

Breathing
Expanding Your Power and Energy
by Michael Sky

Alchemical Healing
A Guide to Spiritual, Physical, and Transformational Medicine
by Nicki Scully

Shamanic Breathwork
Journeying beyond the Limits of the Self
by Linda Star Wolf

The Metaphysical Book of Gems and Crystals
by Florence Mégemont

Inner Traditions • Bear & Company
P.O. Box 388
Rochester, VT 05767
1-800-246-8648
www.InnerTraditions.com

Or contact your local bookseller